Shu-Ha-Ri

Evolving Karate Thoughts

In beloved memory of Palma Diosi Sensei

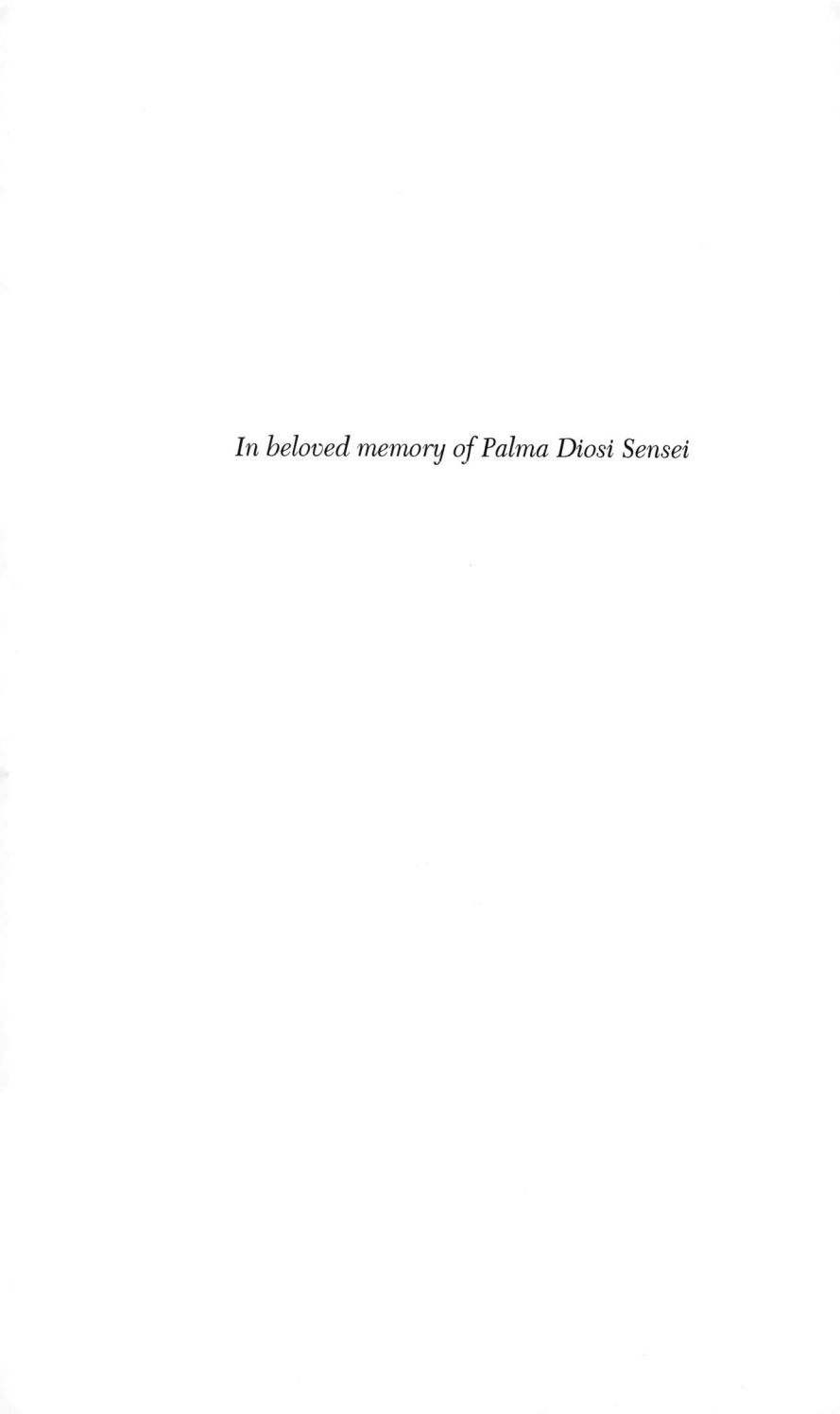

Shu-ha-Ri

Evolving Karate Thoughts

SCOTT LANGLEY

MASON PRESS

First published in 2018 by
Mason Press
Rear of Cullenswood Park
Ranelagh
Dublin 6

All rights © 2018 Scott Lanley

CreateSpace paperback   ISBN: 978-1720680741

Also avaiable as an ebook

All rights reserved. No part of this book may be reproduced or utilised in any form or by any means electronic or mechanical, including photocopying, filming, recording, video recording, photography, or by any information storage and retrieval system, nor shall by way of trade or otherwise be lent, resold or otherwise circulated in any form of binding or cover other than that in which it is published without prior permission in writing from the publisher.

The right of Scott Lanley to be identified as the author of the work has been asserted by him in accordance with the Copyright, Designs and Patents Act 1988.

Cover design by Gareth Jones, www.gazjonesdesign.com
Typeset and layout by Dinky Typesetting and Design

Contents

Prologue — viii

Introduction — x

Chapter One	*Yoko Geri Keage – The New Generation*	13
Chapter Two	*Kokutsu-dachi – The Awkward Stance*	19
Chapter Three	*Shu-Ha-Ri Part I*	25
Chapter Four	*Sempai-Kohai System*	31
Chapter Five	*Sod This for a Game of Soldiers*	36
Chapter Six	*Tube Training – Making Karate Harder*	50
Chapter Seven	*The Snap of Karate*	58
Chapter Eight	*The Snapping Shoulder*	65
Chapter Nine	*The Control of Karate*	70
Chapter Ten	*Zenkutsu-dachi & the Wobbly Knee*	76
Chapter Eleven	*Shotokan: Best of Both Worlds*	83
Chapter Twelve	*Vintage Character vs Modern Technique*	88

Chapter Thirteen	*Ladder to Success*	92
Chapter Fourteen	*Kata – The Algebra of Karate*	97
Chapter Fifteen	*The Straightening of Karate*	105
Chapter Sixteen	*Take a Deep Breath*	114
Chapter Seventeen	*Shapeless Karate*	119
Chapter Eighteen	*New-Fangled Kata*	125
Chapter Nineteen	*Onwards and Upwards*	130
Chapter Twenty	*Connections*	136
Chapter Twenty-one	*Shu-Ha-Ri Part II*	144
Chapter Twenty-two	*Thin Yellow Line*	152
Chapter Twenty-three	*Myths*	156
Chapter Twenty-four	*Post-Modernism*	159
Chapter Twenty-five	*Multiverse*	164
Chapter Twenty-six	*The Bubble*	167
Chapter Twenty-seven	*Micro vs Macro*	170
Chapter Twenty-eight	*Structural vs Social Power*	174
Chapter Twenty-nine	*Training Mechanisms*	180
Chapter Thirty	*Karate – Absolutely*	184
Chapter Thirty-one	*10,000 Hours*	188
Chapter Thirty-two	*Finding Zen in Venn*	192
Chapter Thirty-three	*Oss-ification*	197
Chapter Thirty-four	*Practical Karate*	201
Chapter Thirty-five	*Karate-Do*	209

Prologue

Palma and me.

In the spring of 2012 I was sitting in a café near my dojo in Dublin. Chatting to a friend and sipping tea, I looked out of the window to see Palma leading, mother-duck-like, a dozen or so dogi-clad youngsters along the busy street. I showered my friend in Twinings' finest, spluttered a rather ungentlemanly sentiment and rushed back to the dojo to find it empty – and unlocked. When she eventually returned, my thunderous face instantly put her into explanation mode.

It was a beautiful day …'
My look elicited further explanation.
'It was sunny …'
'And?'
'I wanted to share the great weather with the kids, so we went to the park to train.'

She had only been working for me for six months. She had broken some fundamental aspects of our Child Protection Policy. But this was quintessential Palma – words were said, but I could never remain angry with her. She had an innocence and joy about her that seeped osmotically into all our lives in the six years we knew her. She was fiercely loyal, yet social-butterflied around any multi-association competition or seminar. She would skive off hard morning training with a perpetually deflating bike tyre but then train like a demon on her own in the gym. She would giggle, hug and cuddle her way through life, but then in kumite and she turned into a destroyer, giving little quarter to anyone who stood in front of her.

She was the sister I never had. Above all else, she was deeply loved, respected, admired and is now sadly missed.

Introduction

I started writing articles, initially for *Shotokan Karate Magazine*, in 1996. I was a young *sandan* approaching the end of my time at university. I am unsure why I started. Looking back, it is perhaps easy to say that I had a plan to self-promote; to get my name out there, hoping a small section of the karate world would sit up and pay attention.

I often think this is reverse-engineering and reaching a conclusion that isn't entirely accurate. For sure, over the years I have written extensively and much of that has been used to help raise my profile: after all, I am a professional instructor and this is my job ... the only job I have ever had. But what I realised twenty-two years ago is that I simply like writing. I think about karate all the time. My head is filled with little else, so assigning certain ideas to paper almost allows me to move on to other things. In this book I have included pieces that have been written over the last two decades, all very much of their time. I hope you can see an evolution of thought. Some reference my membership to the JKS, others to the WTKO. I haven't changed anything of the substance because I want to express my contemporary thoughts, most of which I still think hold true. The technical articles, I believe, still have merit, not that I would write them in the same way now. It is not that my understanding has changed, just that it's (hopefully) deepened. Either way, please don't read this book from beginning to end as a narrative. That's not what it is. The chronology wasn't the overriding factor in jostling the articles together in the way they are set out, with the exception that the first article was the long-forgotten one published in 1996 and the last one is my latest offering, that will only be published by me here.

I hope you enjoy – and thank you for your donation to the Irish Cancer Society, www.cancer.ie.

ONE

Yoko Geri Keage – The New Generation

Written in the summer of 1996, this was the first article I ever submitted for publication. Looking back now, it must have been the arrogance of being twenty-three years old that made me think I had something to say about karate. Youth is wasted on the young and wisdom is wasted on the old!

My first memory of learning *yoko geri keage* (side snap kick) was being paired up with a friend of mine, hand in hand, facing each other, kicking each other under the armpit. Since that time, I have been in many classes where the instructor has taught *yoko geri keage*. Each time the explanation has been different. Some feel that it is merely a fast, snapping kick, which can be used to attack under opponents' chins and armpits. Others believe it could be used to knock a knife out of the hands of an attacker! And others resign themselves to the impracticality of the kick in any situation.

However, in recent years British karate-ka have had the

opportunity to train under such great instructors as Kagawa Sensei, Aramoto Sensei and the British-based Kato Sensei and in my opinion it is possible to see a shift in emphasis in their instruction.

As I see it the problem with *yoko geri keage*, as many people do it, is that they do not use their hips, so consequently the direction of one's power only goes upwards. If we use *mae geri keage* as a comparison, we can see that if we do not use the hips in a fast, forward-snapping action, then the power of the kick will go upwards, not forward to the target, therefore losing distance and power. This is a mistake often made by beginners, where the lack of hip movement forward prevents the foot from penetrating the target. In fact, most kicks in Shotokan karate derive their power from either the snapping of the hips or the thrusting of the hips, so why should *yoko geri keage* be any different? I have observed many people doing *yoko geri keage* without the use of the hips. They rely on a sharp knee lift, followed by a fast snapping action of the leg upwards, with the foot kicking at a 45-degree angle. This type of kick, although very fast and aesthetically pleasing, lacks power and distance and would not be effective.

Therefore, in order to make *yoko geri keage* effective, it is imperative to use the hips. The idea is quite straightforward, but as many people have long been used to doing the kick without hip use, they often find the change difficult. Nevertheless, it is worth persevering. The principle of using the hips in *yoko geri keage* is very similar to the hip movement in *mawashi geri*. In *mawashi geri* if one was kicking with the right leg, at the moment of *kime*, the right side hip would be snapped forward then back with the snapping action of the foot/leg; *yoko geri keage* is exactly the same. If one was kicking with *yoko geri keage* to the side with the right leg, the supporting left leg must always remain relaxed and slightly bent, (as the supporting leg helps us to rotate and push the hips) with the supporting foot facing forward. As one pulls the right leg up to ready position, so the knee is facing to the side (to the target), one must allow the right side hip to rotate backwards, with a similar feeling to the *hamni* position in *Zenkutsu-dachi*.

Lack of hip rotation and thrust from supporting leg reduces penetration power. The tower is going upwards, not into the target.

As the foot is released in a fast snapping action, keep the right-side hip back until the very end of the kick and then release the hip in a snapping action forward then back again (like *hanmi – shomen – hanmi* in *Zenkutsu-dachi* and the hip snap in *mawashi geri*).

Correct preparation is vital...

Shu-Ha-Ri – Evolving Karate Thoughts

Like all snap kicks the hip movement in *yoko geri keage* must be left until the very end of the technique to gain maximum power and distance. The key to maximising the power of this kick is to synchronise the hip movement with the push of the supporting leg. As mentioned before, the supporting leg must remain relaxed and bent throughout the kick. However, at the moment of *kime* the leg must be used to push the body into the direction of the target, thus generating penetration power. At the same time, one must rotate the hip so that they push – snap the foot further forward into the target. If these two things are done simultaneously then a line of power is formed from the ground into the target.

Release the right leg but keep you hip back.

Keep supporting leg bent.

Shu-Ha-Ri – Evolving Karate Thoughts

The term 'line of power' is used to describe the principle, fundamental to all karate techniques, whereby one's foundations – stance – uses the floor to push the power into the target in a direct line. For example, in *oi zuki* the back leg pushes straight, so pushing the hips and the punching arm straight to target in one line of power from the ground to the target.

Rotate hips and thrust supporting leg at impact.

Just before the kick reaches full extension, rotate the right hip and push supporting leg.

If this is done successfully one's power no longer travels upwards, but instead travels forward. If you would like to check this have someone hold a football and attempt to kick it with *yoko geri keage*. If the ball goes upwards you are kicking with the top of the foot and doing it wrong. If the ball travels horizontally in the direction of the line of power, then you are kicking with the side of the foot or heel and doing it right.

This way of doing *yoko geri keage* also enables the power of the kick to travel along the leg and out of the heel like *yoko geri kekomi*, making the foot kick at a horizontal position rather than at 45 degrees, as many people do when not using their hips. *Yoko geri keage* can become a very powerful technique with the speed of *mae geri keage* and the power of *yoko geri kekomi*. It is important to master the synchronisation between the snapping hip movement and the push off the supporting leg and, with practice, it can be incorporated within the Shotokan arsenal, rather than being designated the impractical task of kicking knives out of attackers' hands.

At impact, all power travels to the target, forming a line of power from the ground to the opponent.

TWO

Kokutsu-dachi – The Awkward Stance

This article was written late 1999. I'd been in Japan for a few years, I'd had my hair cut and I was desperately trying to be accepted onto the instructors' course.

Kokutsu-dachi (back stance), especially when we first start learning karate, is often considered an awkward, cumbersome and impractical stance. Even after years of training, many karate-ka regard *Kokutsu-dachi* as their slowest, weakest and most unstable stance, as it lacks the strong, penetrating hip movement of *Zenkutsu-dachi*, or the immovable, rooted feeling of *kiba-dachi*. However, is *Kokutsu-dachi* destined to remain relegated to a stance we learn to pass gradings or only apply in kata?

Does not the unique way in which the hips are used teach us body mechanics vital to the maximising of our body's efficiency? And why is it that instructors such as Kagawa Sensei and Osaka Sensei make their *Kokutsu-dachi* look unbelievably solid and powerful?

Shu-Ha-Ri – Evolving Karate Thoughts

We must first look at the stance in situ. The first and most obvious mistake students make is weight distribution. How many times have you heard your instructor say '70 per cent of your weight on the back leg and 30 per cent on the front'? But how many people actually do this? In order to have the 70/30 ratio your right shoulder, hip, knee and foot must be in one complete line. As soon as this line is broken you lose perfect weight distribution.

A simple way to practise this is to stand with the right side of your body against a wall, then slowly lower yourself down into stance. The moment one of the above-mentioned points loses contact with the wall, you have lost correct posture.

This exercise also prevents students from pushing their right knee out and back, putting excess strain on their joints and risking long-term damage. The knee is a hinge joint, and as such should only be bent forwards and backwards, without straining left and right. The left leg points directly forward and should always remain slightly bent. Unlike *Zenkutsu-dachi* where the outer part of the foot points straight forward, in *Kokutsu-dachi* the whole foot points forward down an axis running through the middle. Like the

Stance in situ, right shoulder, hip and knee in line.

foot, the left knee points directly forward too, never moving to either side, exactly like *Zenkutsu-dachi*. And, of course, the left hip and shoulder are in one line (looking from the front), without your backside sticking out, or your body leaning forward.

Once your stance is sorted out, you must then concentrate on hip rotation. Like *Zenkutsu-dachi*, we use hip movement in *Kokutsu-dachi* by pivoting from the front hip.

But unlike *Zenkutsu-dachi*, in *Kokutsu-dachi, hanmi-shomen* is often neglected by instructors, never allowing it to become strong. With practice, *Kokutsu-dachi* hip movement can become as powerful as *Zenkutsu-dachi*. For proof of this one only needs to see Isaka Sensei here in Tokyo do *makiwara* training in *Kokutsu-dachi*.

To perform *hanmi* the hip should be at a complete right angle to the back leg and should have the feeling of squeezing your abdomen/groin area against the side of your inner right thigh. You should also have the feeling of pulling the groin/abdomen area up, so your rear does not stick out. The left (front) hip should be relaxed, so that when you pull the right-side hip back, the action doesn't pull the left leg and knee to one side.

Once in this position, changing to *shomen* is similar to the way we do it in *Zenkutsu-dachi*. Simply push the right-side hip forward whilst pivoting around the left-side hip (because the hip is a ball-and-socket joint, it allows the hip and thigh to move forward without changing the knee and lower-

Maintaining stance, twist the hips and torso into the punch

leg position). At this time the right-side hip must be relaxed so as not to pull the right knee in with the hip movement. To prevent this, you must imagine pushing against the knee.

It is important to note here that if this hip movement is done properly then the right shoulder, hip and knee line (mentioned above) is broken and so, too, is the 70/30 per cent weight distribution. However, I feel it is an often misunderstood concept that within all stances, weight changes, from *hanmi* to *showmen*, as part of the power generation. Without the linear movement back and forth we only have a twist, which is only half the potential power. And, as long as the position from the knees down remains solid, the stance is good.

Once the stance is sorted out, it is then important to concentrate on the movement. The back leg in *Kokutsu-dachi* can act like a spring, much more than the back leg in *Zenkutsu-dachi*. Therefore, a lot of speed and power can be generated when moving forward.

From *hanmi* to *shomen* it is important to use the back leg to push the body forward in a linear motion. Any rounded movement by the arms and legs will only act to slow you down. At the halfway point it is obviously important to keep the same height. Equally important is to keep the weight on the same leg (*jiku ashi*) for as long as possible whilst moving forward into stance. Too many students allow their weight to move too far forward and then pull it back when they execute the block. When you execute a technique, whether a block, punch or strike, all power must be going forward – not forward only to be pulled back at the moment of *kime*. To do this it is important to keep your left knee as well as both hips pointing forward for as long as possible whilst the right leg is moving forward into position. This can only be done by keeping the weight on the left leg. This position should be held until the moment of *kime*, depending on the flexibility of your ankles. Then in the moment of *kime* you should push your right hip forward (as well as 30 per cent of your weight) with your hand technique to complete the movement.

On no account should you feel that your weight moves forward as your right leg goes out, only to be pulled back on the moment of *kime*.

Of course, moving back is of equal importance, but students often find it awkward and slow to pull the front leg backwards. This is because it is awkward to pull the front leg back. We should use the front leg, which is always slightly bent, to push back and create enough momentum to initiate the step, squeezing the inner thigh muscles and allowing the leading hip to pull back, taking the body the remainder of the way. Doing it this way, there is no need to lean forward, putting extra weight on the front leg in order to push back to the halfway point. Once at the halfway position, moving into stance should be as linear as possible. Allow the stepping leg to move back and the moment it touches the ground, pull the hip back, rotating around the front hip to complete the stance, ensuring the back knee is not pulled too much back, and the shoulder, hip, knee and heel

Half-way stage to stepping forward into shuto uke.

line is maintained. Once these points have been practiced it is possible to learn how to use *Kokutsu-dachi* effectively and incorporate it into your arsenal of techniques.

Kokutsu-dachi is great for teaching students how to generate movement and power by the contraction and expansion of the hips, but we will never gain anything from *Kokutsu-dachi* unless we learn the basic body mechanics first.

THREE

Shu-Ha-Ri Part I

I wrote this article a few years after returning from Japan, maybe in 2005. It was one of my first forays into writing about the political and philosophical aspects of our art – whilst in Japan I never really had much time to ponder such matters. I returned to the UK and Ireland when karate was in a state of great flux. Enoeda Sensei had died only a few years before, there was great change in the air and I wanted to make my mark.

Shu-Ha-Ri is a phrase used in Japanese to describe the three stages of one's development. Shu (to protect or to obey), the first phase, describes the first steps; the acquisition of knowledge. Ha (to frustrate) describes the internalisation of that knowledge, making the leap from learning a system to using it in a natural way. Ri (freedom), the last, describes mastery of the system, making it your own and going beyond the limits of the system by pushing the envelope. These stages are seen as the natural path of development and are an integral part of any Eastern learning process.

I believe that for the karate-ka, knowing and thinking about 'how to develop' is just as important as technical development itself. Although, when you start karate this is easy. Everyone is aiming for *shodan*, that coveted black belt: you want to be like one of the guys at the end of the line. Instructors simply have to teach the range of techniques, the various kata and the sets of kumite that make up the Shotokan system. So, by *shodan*, a karate-ka has probably learnt every technique in the system, what more is there to learn? A few kata? However, when *shodan* is attained sensei often start dealing exclusively in clichés:

'Black belt is just the beginning!'

'You have only just started.'

'Now you can start learning.'

And in every way they are correct – how to develop suddenly starts to get increasingly more difficult. *Shodan* just means 'first level'. It is saying that that person is competent at all basic techniques, basic kumite and basic kata. It is at this point that developing one's karate becoming increasingly difficult.

If the instructor follows a traditional, Japanese-based syllabus, *jiyu* kumite is not used in gradings until after *shodan*. From *shodan* to *sandan*, areas like *jiyu* kumite and the more advanced kata can be practised and learnt. All the time the finer nuances of Shotokan technique can be refined and honed. At third dan, karate-ka are considered junior instructors – complete with all the skills a Shotokan karate-ka should have. There may be a few more *kata* that need to be learnt, but the bio-mechanics that make up those *kata* should have already been well developed. From *shodan* to *sandan*, one's development may not be as controlled and dictated to as with beginner to *shodan*, but there certainly is a structure in place to follow.

So from *sandan*, what are karate-ka supposed to do? Just continue repeating the same formulaic karate sessions they have been doing for the last ten to fifteen years? How are they to develop if technically they have already honed their craft? And how do they go from a good understanding of *karate waza* to a mastery of *karate waza*?

In the JKS GB & Ireland we have been very lucky over the last couple of years to have had high-quality karate-ka join our ranks. At the moment I am thinking of two in particular. Both are *Yondan* and came to the JKS from other British-based karate associations with Japanese chief instructors. Both are of a very high standard and could easily be described as having a deep understanding of the Shotokan system. However, having got to know them and their karate, it was surprising to see how little they had been allowed to develop past the standard Shotokan system. In so many ways they were like clones of their previous instructors. They had never been given the freedom or confidence to find their own way in Shotokan karate.

Before we go any further I would like to describe what happens in Japan and use that as a comparison to what happens in the West. In Japan, when someone is awarded *sandan* they take on their own responsibility for their development. This is not an explicit thing, much more something that comes from the culture and set-up of the large organisations there. For example, from *sandan*, karate-ka are considered junior instructors (like I have mentioned). With that comes a certain responsibility. They are allowed to do *kyu* examinations for their students on behalf of the organisation. There is limited

Shu-Ha-Ri – Evolving Karate Thoughts

interference from the hombu/organisation headquarters to the dojo. Therefore, the junior instructors are encouraged to find their own way and the way of their dojo. That is not to say that there is no input from the hombu, just that the dojo is not being dictated to by the hombu. Support is there when they need it, but the headquarters has confidence in the grades that are given out and at *sandan* level and above it is believed that karate-ka are capable of developing a dojo and the students therein.

This mindset is continued for the development of the karate-ka after *sandan*. For *yondan* and above of course they must know all the kata, but beyond that there is no grading syllabus. However, what they must show is something unique. That can be in the form *jiyu* kumite or it may be in the form of self-defence. It can even be in the form of a presentation of how you would teach a certain technique and apply it to kumite. The point is that the grading panel is looking for progress and a sign that the person grading has developed beyond the basic aspect of Shotokan karate, developing their own way. Of course, that is not to say that they have left the Shotokan system behind – they have merely used this system (as a solid foundation) to progress to greater and greater levels

In the West this doesn't seem to happen. The old analogy of the nail having constantly to be hammered down to kept it smooth to the surface is often used. (*Deru kugi wa utareru*: 'The nail that sticks out gets hammered down.') Karate sensei have to push their students down to stop them from becoming arrogant or out of control; but surely this is for the young student, still finding their way within the karate world? However, I have seen fourth, fifth even sixth dans who are treated (in the way they are taught) like *shodans*.

Stifled and restricted by their sensei, they are not allowed to develop and cultivate their karate. Why is this?

I think a big mistake was that early on in the history of Shotokan karate in the UK, Ireland and maybe the rest of Europe, the number of grading examiners was limited. Initially, due to a shortage of experienced sensei and an abundance of students, sensei as low as *shodan* and *nidan* were doing *kyu* gradings. As the number of black belts increased in the country, the same small number of examiners kept a stranglehold on the right to do *kyu* gradings. Eventually, even karate-ka ranking *godan* and *rokudan* were prevented from doing *kyu* gradings by the very same people who have been doing gradings since they were *shodan* and *nidan*.

The reasons for this can be debated another time, but I think the consequences of this decision have been far-reaching within British and Irish karate. Unlike Japan, junior instructors were never given that freedom to express themselves through their karate. Flamboyance was encouraged, if not expected, at the high level end of competition kumite; but for the average dojo instructor there was little they could do. The result is a large number of good solid karate-ka who have never been encouraged or allowed to make Shotokan karate their own.

Going back to Japan I have trained with many great sensei. Of course, most of them have been through the instructors' course. But the instructors' course merely gives us a boost. There is nothing special about it; it just gives us a head start. Having said that, I have trained with many instructors in Japan who have never done the instructors' course. Nagaki Sensei 7th dan JKS, Yagi Sensei 6th dan JKS and Kondo Sensei 6th dan JKS are all brilliant examples of what I am talking about. None of them have done the instructors' course, none of them are world-famous karate instructors, but all of them are brilliant and unique. They have taken the Shotokan system and made it their own. And there are many examples of these types of sensei in Japan.

When I look around I think it is a shame that many good and talented *sandan* and *yondan* Europeans are not allowed to develop and cultivate their karate like their counterparts in Japan. Whether it will take a change in attitude or a change in the financial structuring of organisations, there is no reason why Western countries cannot produce unique, individual karate-ka. It does happen on occasions, but this tends to be the exception rather than the rule. And those that do develop are often forced out to form their own groups, unable to work within the existing organisational framework.

Senior instructors and senior students should really think about 'how to develop'. From *sandan* and above karate must go beyond the physical of 'how can I move faster?' and 'how can I hit harder?' as this is merely the surface level of karate. From *sandan*, karate-ka should be looking at 'How can I make this karate mine?'

FOUR

Sempai-Kohai System

This article was written in about 2003. I had returned from Japan the year before and the subtle lessons I had learnt there had changed my perception of how things were done in Europe. It was also at a time I was writing Karate Stupid. Each chapter of the original manuscript started with a short story told in real time. During that period, most of my articles started in a similar way.

It's December 2001 and I am sitting in a bar in Tokyo drinking beer with my *sempai*, Takashi Yamaguchi. We have been here for a few hours and I have been diligently pouring drinks, ordering food and generally making sure that his glass is always between the half- and three-quarter-filled level. We are chatting about this and that, but I can never really neglect my duties.

After a further hour or so it is time for the last train, plus I fly back to the UK tomorrow for Christmas, so I have to get home. Yamaguchi Sempai speaks to the waitress for the first time that evening. He asks for the bill. I hurry to get his shoes and have them ready at the door. I wait outside and as he leaves I thank him for the evening. He says no problem as he returns his considerably lightened wallet to his back pocket.

Two days later I am sitting in a restaurant in London with another *sempai*, Ian Mason. We are enjoying a few drinks and talking about Japan. Ian has been to Japan many times in his thirty years of training and is interested to hear about the instructors' course. My years in Japan have taught me well and I am yet again a good *kohai*, ordering drinks, pouring beer and making sure my *sempai* is well; this type of behaviour is commonplace in our dojo. The night progresses along and by closing time we are ready for home. Ian calls the waitress over and asks for the bill. She returns with it quickly, Ian picks it up, studies it and then turns to me.

'That'll be £30 each, I guess.'

I duly hand over the money and we head home.

***

I think in the West there is a basic misconception about what the correct *sempai-kohai* relationship should be. The relationship is one of mutual respect and care. The *sempai* takes care of the *kohai* in many ways. Some subtle, maybe working behind the scenes to make sure the *kohai* has good opportunities or advantages. Some not so subtle, always picking up the tab in restaurants or giving the *kohai* a smack in the dojo when they are slacking. In return the *kohai* takes care of the *sempai*. Discreet gestures, maybe making sure you walk ahead and call the elevator before the *sempai* arrives (Asai Sensei never waited for an elevator: by the time he arrived, a junior had already walked ahead, called one and stood holding the door open for him) or filling up the endless glass of beer. Far less subtle actions are at times acting like a servant, making sure bags are carried, doors opened and dogi washed. But whether you like the system or not, it is above all else balanced. The *sempai* supports and respects the *kohai* and the *kohai* acknowledges this by constant support and unwavering loyalty. Plus, the system is self-reproducing. The *sempai* will never hold a door open for the *kohai*. And if you stay in the system long enough, the *kohai* becomes *sempai*, with *kohai* of their own. You then have someone to pour drinks, order food and fetch your shoes. The only problem is then that the new *sempai* must pick up the tab – support them whenever possible.

A few *sempai* in the west have been slightly selective in their understanding of this system. I know of a dojo with an active social life: in the pub the lowest grade always must go to the bar and order drinks. Whoever's round it may be gives the money to the new white belt and they scamper to the bar and back, but when it comes to the white belt's round then they must pay. The *sempai* of the dojo have missed the point. In my own experience, similar to the initial story of my *sempai* in London, I know quite a few who have been somewhat discriminatory when applying the rules of the system. Maybe this is inevitable as we don't live in the strict, regimented society that Japan can sometimes be.

Certainly in the UK we are not without a strict hierarchy system. From the Royal Family down, we are used to knights, lords, barons and counts. Even in parts of South Yorkshire and Cumbria the colloquial use of 'thee' and 'thou' is still common place. Both meaning you, one implies formality and seniority of the person addressed, the other implies informality acceptable with a subordinate. The UK is no stranger to a *sempai–kohai* relationship. So why is it that the Japanese system is so often misused?

Shu-Ha-Ri – Evolving Karate Thoughts

I think the answer is twofold. First, the system is often misused in Japan as well. From office workers being unable to leave their desks until the boss has left (despite having nothing to do), to the extreme of freshers dying at the hands of their university karate club *sempai*, Japan is not without uncaring, selfish, even psychopathic *sempai*. But on the whole these *sempai* are often isolated and cut off from the group. The multitude of subtle actions that are carried out for *sempai* aren't for these type of seniors. The superficial, easily visible actions are, but it stops there; it is no longer a two-way system. Of course, the same misuse of the system exists in the West, although this only goes part way to explain why in the West so many *sempai* miss the point. I think another contributing factor was who we learnt the system from. Many Japanese instructors left Japan and set up in Western countries. Treated like gods on their arrival, I suspect it was difficult to maintain the balance that must be part of any system. With god-like deference, students supported the sensei and expected nothing in return apart from good karate – that was enough. As those students then became *sempai* and sensei and the system was broken and imbalanced, always bound to be a watered-down version of the original.

Is it important? Do we need to use such a system? Well, we could argue that it is intrinsic to karate itself. We use language that subtly speaks of the system: sensei, dojo, dogi, karate-do all imply we are trying to find the way, moving from junior to senior to master. A second argument could be that, without the strictness of such a system, we cannot hope to learn self-discipline and control; essential for anyone who is training in a martial art.

Ultimately it doesn't matter if you use the system or not. It's a personal choice. What is important is that if you do opt into the system you must accept all the facets of it, not just the good ones! The true system is balanced and it is up to the *sempai* to keep it that way.

FIVE

Sod This for a Game of Soldiers

It had been many years since I had read this article – in fact my copy had long been lost to a now-defunct floppy disk clean out. I must thank Simon Bligh and John Cheetham for tracking it down and sending me a copy. It was written at the end of 2002 and the initial few paragraphs are the start of chapter four of Carpe Diem'd Out, which was edited, cajoled and transformed into chapter three of Karate Stupid.

*Hindsight is 20/20 vision, so it is easy to see that this article was instrumental in kickstarting my career. It unleashed the Scott Langley brand upon the karate world – God help us! But now it doesn't even sound like me. I hardly think of my time in Japan now, let alone am I capable of mustering up the enthusiasm to write something about it. That said, it was nice to revisit that part of my past, a bit like discovering a distant cousin: I can see the family resemblance, but there has been a certain amount of divergence since the long-forgotten common ancestor. A striking point is the harshness of the article, or, should I say, the lack of concern of the JKS when it was published. I use their real names: it never went **through** the stringent legal process that my books underwent and I can feel how raw it* *all is to the poor author. Yet the JKS never batted an eyelid. I guess at the time the group was still in its infancy and my personal stock with my sempai still charted high. I hope you enjoy this article as it re-emerges from the dark for one more publication.*

16 March 2000

Last week Kagawa Sensei gave me the nod – my official invitation to become *kenshusei* (trainee instructor). First I have to take the test and I'm making my way to the brand-new, purpose-built facility only twenty minutes from my house. So close. How great is that? [I later came to think quite the opposite.] I haven't been there before, so as I approach the dojo I'm looking forward to seeing the new place. [God, how could I have been so naive.] I'm a little worried about what I will have to do. I know it will be one kata (no problem) and a little kumite ... Urm, that will be a bit tough, as last week Koike Sensei gave me a hard time at the dojo, and I'm thinking it was a taster of what's to come. He actually hit me full force in the stomach. [Oh, ignorance is bliss.] I arrive at Sugamo, and for the very first time I am eagerly strolling the five-minute walk to the dojo. This is it! I have finally made it. [Jeez, I'd only just made it to the starting line.] I enter the dojo and all the sensei are there: Asai, Kagawa, Ishimine, Kanayama, Yamaguchi, Koike, and about four I have never seen before. They look tough, though. I give a deep bow and a friendly smile. A bit of an ice-breaker, never fails. [I cringe at my stupidity.] I'm told to change, and I walk into the locker

SHU-HA-RI – EVOLVING KARATE THOUGHTS

room and am confronted with a young and fresh-looking lad. I give him a hearty '*osu*', realising he is Inada, my fellow trainee instructor, my *doki*. He looks a friendly fellow and although he is growling rather than smiling at me, I put it down to nerves; after all we're both going to take this test. I shake his hand and he is reciprocating with a two-handed handshake. That's what I like to see, a healthy respect for his *sempai* – after all, I am one dan higher and five years his senior!

We're back in the dojo now and the panel of examiners are sitting at the front, awaiting our performance. Asai and Kagawa sensei are flanked by the four unknowns. Ah, it's a good job I gave them all a friendly smile. Best to be on the good side of these guys.

I've done my kata, *Sochin*. No problems. I didn't get any nods of approval, but Inada only did *Bassai Dai*, and he wasn't too hot at that. So next is kumite. I'm suddenly noticing a change of mood. Asai Sensei, who has seemed almost bored until this point, is now looking alert, like a predator suddenly getting the scent of blood. [How right was I?] OK, first *Inada* ... here goes. Don't want to give him too much of a hard time – he is my *doki*, after all.

Oh my God! What the hell was that?

I'm on the floor, I feel blood trickling down from my nose *and* gushing from my bottom lip. How could I have been hit in the nose and the mouth at the same time? He must have fists the size of plates. Mind you, that's presuming it was a punch, it could have been a foot, I didn't really see it. Ishimine Sensei comes over and tells me to get up and continue. No, no, I'm injured, there's been some sort of mistake. Inada has hit me without using control. That's not allowed, is it?

'*Get up!*'

Oh sorry, my mistake. Obviously I'm already brain-damaged, because without saying a word – like 'What the hell's going on?' – I'm back on my feet, waiting for more. Straight out of the 1960s Batman series, BLAM, I'm on the floor again, looking up at the ceiling, thinking, I do Shotokan karate – you know, semi-contact? I hear the word '*Yame*'. Oh, thank God, it's all over. I struggle to my feet, bow and begin to walk off.

As I do, a guttural Japanese voice commands me to stay. I turn around, and I'm facing Koike Sensei. Oh, that's OK. He's my friend, we drink together. [My lord, the naivety.] WHACK. This just isn't cricket. I'm on the ground again, looking up at Koike Sensei, hoping my innocent eyes will induce some compassion in him.

CRACK. He's just encouraged me to stay on the dojo floor a little longer. What the hell is going on here?

I hear '*Yame*' again, and quickly Koike is replaced by Yamaguchi. Gone is the title *sensei*, as the only thing they are teaching me now is how to bleed. Yamaguchi is just blinding fast and all I remember is at one point Ishimine, who is refereeing this fight ['Refereeing' would imply we are playing by competition rules] kindly grabs the back of my dogi, thus preventing me from going head first over the table where Asai, Kagawa and the four dignitaries are sitting and who, incidentally, haven't batted an eyelid at the grotesque show of violence that is taking place in front of them. Eventually '*Yame*' is called again. [Is there a sweeter word in the English I mean Japanese language? I think not.] I'm virtually dragged to the sidelines, where I am allowed to watch Inada do his two blood-free bouts. [Why aren't they knocking the living daylights out of him, too?] But all I can really think is, *I've just found hell on Earth and it is kenshusei.*

Kenshusei, usually translated as 'instructor's course',

actually refers to the participant of the course, the trainee instructor. Since its inauguration in 1955, the JKA, and since the split, the JKS too, have had thousands of people enter the

Scott Langley 4th Dan – JKS Instructor

course. Out of these thousands only about a hundred have successfully passed the course, and out of this hundred only four had been foreigners. For two years I trained relentlessly at the JKS headquarters with sensei and *sempai* like Asai, Kagawa, Yamaguchi, Kanayama, Ishimine, Koike and of course my *doki*, Inada (the current 70 kg kumite world champion) and in April 2002 I became the fifth non-Japanese to successfully complete the course. So, as I have been given an almost unique insight into this infamous course, I thought I would try to dispel some of the mystery and myth that surround it.

Let's start with the training – after all that is what *kenshusei* is all about, right? Well actually no, it isn't, but the training is a good place to start ... Every weekday the *kenshusei* (both first and second years) would arrive at the dojo first. The normal morning class started at 10.30 am, so arriving an hour beforehand was the best way one reached the dojo before one's *sempai*. Arriving late was a sure way to bring their wrath upon oneself, something that had to be avoided at all costs. One of the senior instructors of the hombu would teach the morning class, and the *kenshusei* were expected to join in. Before entering the course, I always thought that these classes were really tough. Being taught by a senior sensei and having the *kenshusei* breathing down my neck was the perfect morning wakeup call. Once on the course these classes became so easy... Everything, I discovered, is relative.

The morning class finished at 11.30 am. We had thirty minutes to get ready for *shidoin geiko* (instructors' training), which started at 12 pm. Normally the *kenshusei* were left alone, but if one's *sempai* felt frisky, or one had stepped out of line during the previous hour ... day, week or month, then a *sempai* would invite you to do *jiyu* kumite. When doing this *jiyu* kumite you always had to find the right balance between trying to beat him, without actually hitting him. He could, and did, hit you as hard as he wanted, but control must always be used with one's *sempai*. Many times I would fail in finding the right balance and would start *shidoin geiko* covered in blood – my own blood that is. After the warm-ups we would do about one hour of non-stop basics. A hundred *gyaku zuki* left and right, a hundred *mae geri* left and right. Maybe fifty *yoko geri* left and right, before moving onto normal *idou kihon*, going up and down the dojo. We never did any 'advanced' combinations, just simple *kihon* like *age uke – gyaku zuki* or *mae geri-oi zuki*. Once, halfway through my second year we did *soto uke yoko empi – uraken – gyaku zuki*. It was literally the most interesting combination I had done in years ... I smiled for a week! *Kihon* was followed by kumite. We only ever did *gohon* kumite, *jiyu ippon* kumite and *jiyu* kumite. Sometimes we practised kumite drills, especially using rubber tubing for resistance training. However, I never remember doing *sanbon* or *ippon* kumite; it was just never taught. Kumite would last for about thirty or forty minutes, and then we would usually finish with kata. Kata training was very basic. The *sempai* would count and everyone would do it, maybe once slowly and then three or four times, speed and power. I don't ever remember practising *bunkai*. And that would be the routine. Every day, Monday to Friday. *Kenshusei* were also expected to help out one's *sempai* with evening classes, attend weekend technical seminars and compete on a regular basis, so basically we rarely got a rest.

Sounds pretty monotonous, doesn't it? Well it was, who said getting good was interesting? We trained full-time, we didn't teach full-time, which I feel a lot of people in the West mistakenly believe to be the same. No, we were expected to put all our energy into training. Learning how to teach was no part of the course. Nobody told me that before I entered.

However, to say that was all the course consisted of is a big mistake. Training hard is one thing, but training hard under extreme pressure is a different thing entirely. The *kenshusei* course is like stretching an elastic band. In order to achieve a permanent change one must stretch the band far beyond the required length, knowing that when it springs back, it will have been lengthened forever. The same thing is done to *kenshusei*. They are pushed to their extreme, then they are pushed beyond it, and they are pushed until breaking point. It is a cliché to talk about being pushed to one's breaking point, but believe me it is possible. And it would be nice to think that the sensei have a sense of one's limits and push you just to the very edge but I don't believe that is so. Being a *kenshusei* graduate is being part of a very exclusive club. In order to enter the club you not only have to be pushed to one's limits, but those limits must also be as high as everyone around you. For every graduate of the course there are many who have tried and failed. They, too, pushed themselves to the edge, unfortunately most of them were then helped over the edge by their *sempai*.

At the beginning of my second year two new people started the course. Inada and I were ecstatic to have *kohai* at long last. I was happy as there would be more cannon fodder for my *sempai* to feed upon; Inada was happy as he had two people who he was allowed

Scott Langley spent five years training in Japan, here at the JKS Headquarters in Sugamo

to beat up! Our *kohai* were Doi from Japan and Ricardo from Mexico. The year before Doi had been the captain of Teikyo University (Kagawa Sensei's university and current national champions) and had recently been selected for the All-Styles National Team. Ricardo was a naive 26-year-old who, after winning everything that Mexico could offer, had been sent by his sensei to Japan to enter the instructors' course. Doi was certainly one of the best fighters in Japan and Ricardo was very fast, strong and determined. They had the talent and opportunity to become the best in the world. Ricardo lasted three weeks and Doi lasted eight weeks. Why? Who knows, I just remember being very jealous of them that they had been able to escape.

So how do they push you? I think a perfect illustration of this happened one day in the early summer of 2001. Kagawa Sensei had us doing kumite combination training. It was particularly hot (37°C) and as a way to help me acclimatise to training in such extremes Yamaguchi Sempai had kindly turned off the air-conditioner – he was so thoughtful. We had been training non-stop for 90 minutes, and I could feel the energy draining quickly from out my feet. We had moved on to kumite drills (*kizami zuki – gyaku zuki – oi zuki*). Paired up, I had to attack whilst my partner, Doi, stepped back blocking and finishing off with *gyaku zuki* full force to my stomach.

After a further ten minutes of doing this I was spent. I could barely hold up my arms. Kagawa Sensei came and stood behind me, told me to do it again, but this time to do it faster and stronger. I did, but I had no energy, I could barely stand, never mind attack Doi whilst looking convincing. When I finished, Kagawa Sensei, without warning, hit me full force in the face. I fell like the proverbial sack of spuds and started to see a mixture of stars and blood. I don't remember how hard, but I do recall getting kicked in the ribs whilst I was down, and being told to do it again, but this time with spirit. Now, I hope you're not thinking, 'What a wimp.' Honestly, I had given it my all, but still I was faced with two choices: A: explain to Kagawa Sensei in my most polite Japanese that in actual fact that had been my best attempt and, hoping to appeal to his reasonable side, any further attempt would be rather counter-productive, or B: get up, dig deep, find some energy and try to knock Doi's teeth down his neck. Fearing the wrath of Kagawa Sensei, I chose B. You can always find energy from somewhere when faced with further beatings. I did the drill, achieving my goal of finding more energy, but failing to knock Doi's teeth out (which is good as he only had about three left). Kagawa Sensei grunted and then shuffled off, muttering something about foreigners under his breath, leaving me to slowly bleed all down the front of my dogi.

It's a nice story, isn't it? And it does have a point. Without that pressure, I would never have found the energy to push myself that little bit further. After that day I always knew that I could do a little more, even when every inch of my body screamed out otherwise. It was this continuous pushing by my sensei and *sempai* that allowed my karate elastic band to be stretched to the extreme. They knew, once I finished the course, my karate would have been 'stretched' forever.

Another part of this elastic-band theory was the *sempai–kohai* relationship. It was unbelievably strict. One infringement of the rules would lead to a severe beating; but you only learned the rules by trial and error, no one ever told you. It was like when owners of big dogs say things like, 'He'll only bite you if you annoy him' but then don't tell you what annoys him: for example, breathing!

Inside and outside the dojo things had to be just so. During training I would find myself in trouble for counting too fast, for counting too slow, for getting the order of the warm-ups wrong, for losing a fight in a competition or for not saying '*osu*' fast enough.

Outside the dojo I would attract the wrath of my *sempai* for wearing sunglasses, for not running to open a door or call an elevator or for even misunderstanding a blurted-out order in guttural Japanese from a senior who'd had too much to drink. Every discretion would result in a beating. On one occasion (I forget my crime) I was being punished with *jiyu* kumite by Yamaguchi Sempai. I knew he was after my blood, as his fists had been whizzing past my face with shocking closeness – they never bothered hitting me in the stomach. Eventually he got through and gave me an enormous smack to my mouth. He actually put two of my lower front teeth through the part of the mouth that joins my lower lip to my chin (does that have a name?... maybe lipette?) There was a massive, gaping hole after I had unhooked my lip from off my teeth. Again my dogi was covered with blood. At times like this there was always a cathartic release. My *sempai* had got what he wanted and I would clean up the dojo (i.e. the blood I had carelessly spilled on the dojo floor) and be allowed to go home. But on this occasion Yamaguchi *Sempai* wasn't happy. In his bid to knock my head off he had cut his two knuckles on my teeth. He looked at the bloody hole in his hand and then looked at me.

'Scott.' He didn't actually call me Scott, but in the interest of our younger readers ... 'Do you clean your teeth before you come to the dojo?'

'Yes, *sempai*.'

'Well, make sure you clean your teeth every day, as I don't want to get an infection in my hand!' I instantly assured him that I would do as he asked, but at the same time I was thinking: What sort of world do I live in where it is my responsibility to stop my sempai from getting an infection in his hand when hitting my teeth?

I never got a satisfactory answer to that one. All I remember was about three weeks later noticing that Yamaguchi Sempai's hand still hadn't healed, whilst my lipette had, and I thought to myself: You see, actually I am stronger than he is, as I heal faster! It was just one of the ways that I dealt with the stress. I blatantly deluded myself. I also dealt with the daily stress by throwing up through nerves every morning, developing obsessive compulsive disorder and becoming a functional alcoholic ... but that's a whole different article. Something we'll leave *Psychiatrists Weekly* to publish.

I don't want to give the impression that I was constantly being beaten up. It felt that way at the time, but no one can ever take such punishment, it was just the constant fear of the punishment. The Chinese define terrorism as 'kill one to scare a thousand'. I'm not saying my sempai were terrorist nor did people die on

Takeshi Yamaguchi, former All Japan Kata and Kumite Champion, Scott Langley's Sempai

Shu-Ha-Ri – Evolving Karate Thoughts

the course (that only happens at the universities), what I am saying is that I never knew when the next beating would come. I had been beaten up before, and I knew I would be again, and it was the not knowing that was the worst part. I was always on edge and it was totally out of my control. The only thing I could do to limit the beating was to train as hard as I could. It was the only power I had, so that is what I did. Therefore, my *sempai* terrorising me had the desired effect – it made my karate better.

Was it worth it? I can honestly say that nothing that I went through during the two years was pointless. Maybe my

We trained full time, not taught full time – there is a difference.

statement before, that my sensei weren't aware or cared about pushing me beyond my limit, was a bit unfair. They did successfully get me through the two years. At times I thought I would never make it, and at times I thought they hoped I would never make it, but I did. The result? I hope my karate is better. It has opened up new opportunities that would never have been available to me without doing the course. I am now resident in Ireland, teaching throughout Europe, but more importantly it gave me a sense of how to train, how to improve and how to keep on pushing myself, and that alone makes it worthwhile.

SIX

Tube Training – Making Karate Harder

I wrote this article in 2003. I think I can confidently say that not many people were doing tube training in Europe before I wrote this ... now I see Facebook videos of karate-ka doing it throughout the world!

It's my first day on the instructors' course. I have no idea what I am going to face. Nerves and fear seem to be the order of the day. I have only ever seen these guys at the front of the class; now I am training alongside them. What makes them so special, so fast and strong? What secrets are they going to share with me in the next two hours; in the next two years?

We finish warming up and Kagawa Sensei simply says 'tubes'. Everyone scurries off and comes back with bicycle inner tubes. I am given one and I see that it is in actual fact four or five inner tubes, which have been cut and tied to make large elastic-band type things. One end is anchored to the wall and we start – an hour of non-stop *kihon* and kumite drills. It is my first experience of tube training and I suddenly realise there are no secrets in karate, only hard work.

※ ※ ※

Before I moved to Japan I had never heard of tube training, let alone been forced to do it. Even when I was training normally at the Hombu Dojo in Tokyo, we never used this particular form of training. However, once on the instructors' course everything changed and tube training became a major part of my training schedule.

I can understand why my sensei waited so long to introduce this form of training. Tubes offer resistance. Resistance is only beneficial to already strong, well-formed technique, so doing this form of training as part of the training regime of the young and/or inexperienced will be counterproductive. However, I believe that there are many karate-ka in the world whose karate would greatly benefit from this form of practice.

As I mentioned before, the actual apparatus is simply four or five bicycle inner tubes that have had the air nozzle cut off and then been tied together end to end to make one large elastic band. Then one end is anchored to a wall (or if you are doing it with a partner, one end can be looped around your partner's waist). The other end is held/attached to yourself and the resistance of the tubing forces you to execute your technique with greater effort. Over time, this training increases speed and strength and then without the tubing you will see improvements in your karate.

Tube training regimes can be devised for the requirements of each individual, and here I will demonstrate a couple of training methods that maximise the speed and power of karate.

Gyaku Zuki

The preparation for gyaku zuki is very simple. Holding the tube in the punching hand, it is important to have the tube horizontal, but not taut. This way, when the punch is started, there is immediate resistance, but not so much that it is impossible to punch.

When the punch is released, you must keep the tube in

the hand, drive from the back heel and snap the hips forward. Allow the hand to return to *hikite* immediately. Tube training stresses the snap in every technique. If you try to thrust or you are tense and stiff in the shoulders, you will be unable to do this type of training.

HIKITE/HIP TRAINING

This training really emphasises a strong snap with the hips and the correct recoil of the *hikite* (pulling) hand. Holding the tube outstretched, with the tube horizontal, but not taut, snap the hip and the hand back to *hikite*. Whilst doing this maintain the correct body posture, paying particular attention to your tailbone. Do not allow your bum to stick out when performing this technique. Snap the hips back into *hanmi*, make the correct tension and then release the arm forward again. The return of the arm forward also emphasises the correct rotation of the fist and screwing action of the arm, in order to make correct *kime* with *gyaku zuki*.

Mae Geri

Attaching the tube securely to your foot can be a little difficult. First, step through the tube, then make a loop with the front of the tube, making a figure 8 shape (small top loop and very large bottom loop). Place the small loop over your foot and pull the tube taut so the cross of the '8' is across the front of your ankle. This should hold the tube in place. Start with your hips square so that you are only concentrating on the knee lift, stomach squeeze and the hips snapping forward. Performing *mae geri* with tubes forces you to concentrate on a sharp knee lift and strong hip snap forward. Also, as the foot is snapped back into stance, the supporting leg must remain slightly bent in order to keep stability.

Kumite Drills

Preparation for kumite drills can be varied. The simplest form is to place the tube around your waist. Driving off the back leg with yori-ashi, the tube resists, which increases speed and power. However, the tube can also be held or attached to the foot, depending on what kumite combination you are practising. When ready, drive forward with the combination. The tube forces you to be smooth and flowing, snapping every technique to maximise power, speed and distance.

I think it is important to stress a couple of points that apply to tube training. I have already mentioned about karate-ka who are very tense in the shoulders when they punch. Of course this applies to all hand techniques and it is very important to snap (rather than thrust) one's technique. *Kime* is only made for a split second and any excess tension will only hinder and slow down the technique. If you practice *kihon waza* with the tubes, it really helps to emphasise snapping *kime*. Then, without the tubes, it is possible to maintain one's form when performing, but still have the feeling of snapping one's *kime* (i.e. at the moment of *kime*, tense the muscles and then immediately relax, whilst still keeping the form).

When performing *mae geri* the habit is to come back into *hanmi* and then start from this position. This should be avoided. If you start from *hanmi* you start to rock backwards and forwards and the effect is like having a running start. By the time you start with the knee lift and stomach squeeze, you already have forward momentum. It may seem easier to kick this way, but it is less effective in regards to training. With this technique (and every other basic technique described above) start from a completely still position. This way the training will build twitch muscle and emphasise fast starting action and a strong snapping technique.

With kumite drills it is important to practise *yori-ashi* only (back foot push). If you start with *yose-ashi* (back foot half step then push) or *okuri-ashi* (back foot to front foot then push), your body already has gained momentum before you meet resistance from the tube. Whenever doing a kumite drill only push off the back leg every time a technique is delivered.

Finally, the best tubing is the Thera-Band silver latex tubing. It has the perfect resistance for this type of training, although it can be a little expensive as you need at least six or seven metres to make one tube. However, the cheap and just as effective alternative is bicycle inner tubes. Often bike shops will have old tubes with punctures that they will give you for free. They may need a good wash before use, but they work just as well.

It is often noted how fast and strong the traditional Japanese karate-ka move. Whilst in Japan my *doki* (class mate) was Yasuhisa Inada (former 70 kg WKF World Champion) and my *kohai* was Shinji Nagaki (current 70 kg WKF World Champion). They both practised kumite drills over and over again with tubes. Like sprinters who practise with small resistance parachutes on their backs, Inada and Nagaki found tube training a great way to increase speed and power. When they took them off and fought normally the result was breathtaking speed and power. We don't all aim to be world champions, but tube training offers an easy and effective supplement to our normal training.

SEVEN

The Snap of Karate

This article was written for Shotokan Karate Magazine in 2005 and was the start of a series of technical articles that really helped me solidify what my core beliefs of karate were.

I remember years ago watching Bruce Lee films. Like many, he was my idol and although he died the year after I was born, I grew up watching his movies over and over again.

When I was twelve I started karate and shortly after my first lesson I remember watching a documentary of Bruce Lee where he talked about kung fu and karate. He said karate was like being hit by an iron bar – 'WHACK' as he mimed using an iron bar to hit someone. 'However,' he continued, 'kung fu is like being hit by an iron bar attached to a chain,' and then he made a noise only Bruce Lee could make, as he mimed the snap of the bar and chain combination. I wish I did kung fu, I thought!

Twenty years later I have come to realise that maybe Bruce

Shu-Ha-Ri – Evolving Karate Thoughts

Lee didn't know everything there was to know about karate. However, I have forgiven him as I have seen many karate-ka who have also failed to see the snap of karate.

Please try this: make a fist and then hold your index finger up, straight. Now, as quick as you can, bring the finger back down to the fist. Now return the finger back to the same place, but with your other hand pull the finger back as far as it will go and then release. Hopefully there will be a difference. With the first exercise the finger is being forced forward by the tension of the muscles. With the second exercise, it is the other hand that is forcing the finger back and when it is released it snaps forward. Because the muscles in the moving finger are relaxed, it moves twice the distance of the previous exercise in less time. This 'snap' of the finger can demonstrate how we should snap all our techniques.

Let me first talk about what I see is inefficient about the way that many people do karate. For the sake of simplicity, I am going to refer to this as the 'Western' style of karate. However, let me assure you, I trained for many years in Japan and I have seen many karate-ka there do techniques in a similar fashion, but this style seems to be more prominent in the West and therefore I will refer to it as the 'Western' style. And that style is tense and stiff, with movements of the arms being forced into place as techniques are executed.

If we take the example of the simple *gedan barai*, people often execute this block in two movements. As they start to move forward from the simple *yoi* position, they bring their arm up so the blocking hand is to the side of their face. That position is then locked as they step forward. As they land, they force their arm/hand down to the blocking position. From the still relaxed *yoi* position, the arm is constantly tense throughout the movement. Even when they land their arm remains tense as it is forced into place. This is how beginners learn the techniques, but I have seen high dan grades do the technique in a similar, stifled, stiff manner.

In order to maintain that locked, prepared position as you move forward, you have to tense your muscles. With tense muscles, you are probably able to get your fist up as far as your ear, but no farther. This tension also causes a blockage of the body's natural power. Then, as the block is executed, the arm is still tense. In the short term it may feel strong, but tension of any muscle makes movement slow and slow movement reduces the power and effectiveness of a technique.

The 'Japanese' style is much more relaxed and, therefore, stronger and faster. We have all been on a course taught by instructors who seem to glide across the floor with so much speed and control and then deliver a fast, strong technique. I have been there, trying to produce the same amount of power, but the more effort I put into it, the less effective it seems to be. How can they make it seem so effortless? I asked myself. But that is it! Less 'effort', less tension is what produces the increased power and snap of their techniques.

Please try this exercise. Stand with your arms outstretched, shoulder blades back, chest open and upper body completely relaxed. Now, with your pectoral muscles, pull your arms in, so they wrap around your body. This is just a fast, snapping exercise. The idea is not to hug yourself and keep hold of your body. The idea is to snap your arms into your body, only to allow them to return (not force them to return) back to the start point. Try this exercise repeatedly, only concentrating on the initial 'snap' of the pectoral muscles, which bring the shoulder blades forward. If you hug yourself (depending on your flexibility) you will probably be able to get your hands to your shoulder blades. If you snap, the relaxed arms/hands will travel farther and faster, with your hands momentarily making it farther around you back. This is how you should execute *gedan barai*.

From a *yoi* position, try moving into *gedan barai*. This time, instead of stopping at the preparation point, try to recreate this snap feeling. Of course, the preparation is different from hugging yourself, although the initial snap and the bringing forward of the shoulder blades is exactly the same. Also, if you are relaxed, you will find that the hand makes is much farther back and goes beyond the ear. Keeping the shoulders and arms completely relaxed (only using the pectorals to prepare) allows you to move in a smooth, unstilted manner. Plus, if you are relaxed enough, your arms will snap back (just like your leg in *mae geri*). As it snaps back, you will be moving into stance and as you finish your technique then you add the split second of *kime* (tension) to produce the final power of the technique.

As beginners it is very difficult to make power with karate techniques. The movements are unusual and clumsy. We are learning to use our bodies in ways that don't make sense. As a result, many people tense their bodies as it is a natural/unlearnt way of creating power. It feels strong and initially produces results, but this over-tension of the body always stifles power when the karate movements are learnt. If you try these two ways of training and compare the tense, two-part movement of the 'Western' style to the constant fluid action of the 'Japanese' style, it becomes obvious that the latter style is superior.

We can then take this principle and apply it to all our techniques. The basic blocks divide into two categories. Out to in (e.g. *age uke* and *soto uke*) and in to out (e.g. *gedan barai* and *uchi uke*). An exercise for the in to out category is the one described above, and for the other category you can practise the opposite. Start with your arms hugging yourself and shoulder blades forward. Concentrating on the back muscles, snap you shoulder blades back and elbows to the side like *yoko empi* (don't allow your arms to become outstretched, you don't want to cause hyper-extension). As they reach their apex, allow the snap to bring them back to the hugging position.

Once you have mastered the 'feeling' of the snap in the exercise, recreate it when you do the blocks. *Gedan barai* has already been described. For *soto uke*, as you prepare, make sure the blocking arm shoulder is brought right back as far as it will go (without hyper-extension) and then the snap will catapult it forward. Again, just at the end add the split second of *kime* to produce the strong, fast, smooth action so characteristic of the 'Japanese' style. (A word of caution: when people practise *soto uke* they are often over-concerned with

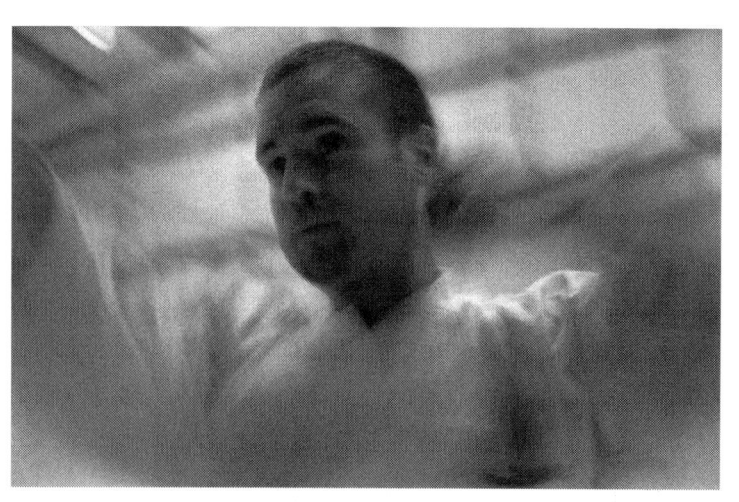

Karate technique must be dynamic, producing snap in everything we do.

where the hand should be in preparation. This is not important. The fist should remain close to the ear. What is important is that the shoulder and shoulder blade is snapped back. If we consider *age uke,* the hand doesn't move, although that is not to say there is no preparation with the blocking arm. The preparation of the shoulder is vital and should feel exactly the same as the *soto uke* preparation.)

There are two further points I would like to make before I conclude this article. The point about the *age uke* preparation is vital to understanding how the relaxed use of the shoulder snap can be used for punching. Just because the hand does not move does not mean that the same body mechanics mentioned above do not come into play. If we consider *oi zuki,* when stepping forward the arm that will deliver the punch does not move. However, the snap of the shoulder should still be used to create a relaxed, fast punch. If you just rely on the arm muscles to force the arm forward it will produce a slow, stifled weak thrust, not a snap.

Secondly, the shoulder is a ball-and-socket joint. So too is the hip. Although the exercises I have mentioned above would not apply to the hip, the hip can be used in a similar way. If you combine the snap of the shoulder with the snap of the hip, it will produce far more power than the forced, stifled approach of the 'Western' style.

I would like to conclude by going back to Bruce Lee. I agree with him, I think kung fu (from what I have seen) is like an iron bar attached to a chain. It has that fluid, non-fixed form to it that is so alien to karate-ka. However, he is wrong about the 'iron-bar karate'. Good karate should never be stiff; although it does have more form than kung fu. I prefer to think of karate as a flexible piece of steel. If you imagine a piece of steel that has been securely anchored at one end with the other end pulled back to its maximum apex, the power that is required is in the pull back. This produces potential power, which is released when the steel is freed and is snapped forward. Because there is no tension on the release, there is no blockage of power. Karate is exactly the same. We always maintain our form, but within that movement, we use the body to snap our techniques into place and use *kime* to finalise the movement.

EIGHT

The Snapping Shoulder

Looking back now at these articles, maybe fifteen years after they were written, reminds me that no one is reinventing the wheel. Having said that, I can see the constant evolution of technique, which is vital for any dynamic, living art. This one was written in 2006 for Shotokan Karate Magazine.

I think first I have to qualify what I mean by 'the snapping shoulder'. I have thought long and hard about what term I could use that would adequately describe this particular movement, but have failed to come up with any comprehensive term. Therefore, I have deferred to those who are in the know. At the Japan Karate Shotorenmei Headquarters Kagawa Sensei always refers to it as the shoulder snap, and consequently, so will I. But please remember it is merely a name for the action, rather than a description of it.

In May 2001 I accompanied Kagawa Sensei on a trip to Manchester, to help teach and translate on a course that had been organised by SKM. It goes without saying that Kagawa

Sensei's technique and teaching style impressed and inspired those in attendance. After the course, talking to the various karate-ka from around the UK, the major topic of discussion was how Kagawa Sensei used and taught the shoulder snap.

What is the shoulder snap? In essence it's very simple and there are three quick exercises that can help to teach your body how to maximise the shoulder's potential. First, stand in *shizentai* and put both hands out making *choku-zuki* position (both fists should be touching side to side). Now, keeping your chest perfectly square-on, and not changing the angle between your chest and left arm, relax your right shoulder and allow your arm to move directly forward, as if it's growing. Now return your right arm back to its previous position and do the same exercise with your left arm. It seems such a simple exercise, but it is remarkable how many people don't use this extra extension when they punch.

The second exercise is equally easy. Simply throw (or imagine throwing) a basketball, with both hands, straightforward. The idea is to keep the elbows tucked in and concentrate on the shoulders 'snap' to push the elbows forward, propelling the ball. This little exercise helps you concentrate on the sharp twitch movement of the shoulder, which acts as the impetus of the punch, plus the follow-through shoulder extension, which provides the greater penetration of the technique.

Once you have mastered the extension of the first exercise and the snap of the second, it is important to loosen up your shoulder. For the third exercise, start with your right leg slightly forward, and your body in a relaxed *hamni* position. You left hand is unimportant, but your right hand should be at the *hikite* position, completely relaxed. Starting from there, perform *age uke*, but without *kime*, solely concentrating on the snap and extension of the shoulder. When performing this shoulder snap think of how you move when you shrug your shoulders. Of course, you are only using your right shoulder at this time, but you should have the same feeling.

The sharp movement upwards of your shoulder should act as an impetus for your blocking arm, allowing your shoulder to produce a greater extension than usual. Once your arm has reached its greatest extension, bring your fist back to *hikite*. Throughout the exercise your arm shouldn't stop or reach a point of *kime*, so as soon as your fist reaches *hikite*, perform *mawashi empi*, going from right to left across your body in a wide, sweeping arc. Again the technique is not so important, just concentrate on the snap and extension of the shoulder that you need to do this technique. This snapping technique should feel like a shoulder barge, a sharp, snapping action forward, again acting as an impetus for the *mawashi empi*.

Finally, as the *mawashi empi* reaches a greater-than-normal extension to the left, snap the shoulder again in the opposite direction, like a reverse shoulder barge, performing *yoko empi* to the right, once again concentrating on the snap and extension of the shoulder. Once you reach maximum extension, allow your fist to return to *hikite*, and repeat the exercise again and again. The three techniques should be performed in one smooth and rounded action, using the shoulder as the impetus for each movement.

This is a very long-winded explanation for a simple little exercise, but believe me we do this exercise forty or fifty times a day with each arm on the instructors' course, and it's very effective for loosening up the shoulder.

Once you have mastered these little ideas, how do you apply them to techniques? Well, I think for many years now we have been overwhelmingly concerned with how to use the hips correctly, and how they should act as the impetus for the punching hand. And rightly so. In fact we can see, certainly with British karate, that about ten to fifteen years ago, it had an almost paradigm shift in thinking, followed by what could be described as an explosion of innovation regarding body pivoting, relaxed back leg, hip rotation in *Kokutsu* and *kiba dachi*, etc. The result of this was an emphasis on hip movement as the impetus for punching. If we use right-hand *gyuku zuki* as an example, we can see that we use the relaxed back (right) leg to snap the right side hip forward (much in the same way as the shoulder snap, after all they are both ball and socket joints), transferring the power to the fist, resulting in *gyaku zuki kime*. Of course, we often concentrate on keeping the elbow tucked in to stop flicking the punch, but rarely have I seen people teach that the elbow should be used to propel the fist forward. If we only concentrate on the hip we neglect a major power source for our punch.

At the start of the punch the shoulder, in a relaxed state, should be snapped forward. Its best to imagine that the power that this generates flows to your elbow, not your fist, pushing it forward. This movement should be allowed to continue until you reach full extension, with the shoulder relaxed forward, and you reach *kime*. When this is done in unison with the hip snap, it's useful to imagine that the hip is propelling the fist forward, whereas the shoulder is propelling the elbow forward. Like most things in karate, imagining the mechanics of your body is vital to achieving the potential of this technique.

Another important key to this idea is not to tense the shoulder when punching. I have seen so many people tense all their shoulder muscles at the moment of *kime*, but if you do this it's impossible to gain the extra penetration. Your shoulder will naturally use and tense the correct muscles it needs on the point of *kime*, without hindering your action by over-tensing. If done correctly, this shoulder extension will bring into play not only the lat muscles, but also the back muscles running down along the spine, which, I feel, is often a part of the body underused by most karate-ka.

Finally, it is important to point out two basic concepts. Firstly, when executing the technique, you must still breathe out, like we do with all techniques. In fact, just because you are trying something new, please don't abandon old, correct principles that you have been practising for years. And secondly, this concept can be applied to any hand technique, whether it is a punch, block, or strike. I have only used *gyaku zuki* and *choku zuki* as examples for this article, but the shoulder snap and extension can improve the power, speed and add several inches reach to any technique; please don't fixate on punching.

I think that this very simple idea is capable of improving both power and penetration of one's technique. And with the simple exercises it is easy to incorporate this principle into one's existing karate. In conclusion, I must point out that the use of the idea should not result in *gyaku-hamni*. *Gyaku-hamni* is an entirely different technique where the upper body and hips continue pivoting so, if punching right-hand *gyaku zuki*, the right side of the body is in front of the left side. The idea that I have just described does not affect the finish position of the hips, upper body or shoulder of the *hikite* hand, it only affects the shoulder of the punching hand.

NINE

The Control of Karate

When I first moved to Ireland – and at the time I was writing these technical articles – I was living with Gayle Kenny PhD. She held a doctorate in philosophy and specialised in the philosophy on the mind. We would speak at length over the dinner table about how the mind developed. I would give my thoughts and she would challenge flaws in my logic. Looking back, it was a valuable part of how my approach to karate developed. I know that this article sprang from one dinnertime conversation.

My instructor once said to me that the moment I walked through the dojo door I was his. To turn up for karate was to give oneself to the sensei for the duration of the class.

Recently I have been reading, albeit on the internet, about people who have given up the trappings of Shotokan karate. They no longer feel the need to use terminology that most of us take for granted as being an essential part of training.

Words like *osu*, sensei and *Zenkutsu-dachi* have been dismissed as irrelevant and been replaced by the English 'equivalent'. These people have claimed that a word is just a word, and each country should use its native tongue when teaching karate.

Members of the other side of the argument have counter-claimed that this takes something away from what we are doing, and have posed the question: 'At what point do changes like these alter what we are doing into something that is no longer karate?'

It is an interesting point and I began to think about the importance, if there is any, of using Japanese terminology in the dojo. Why do we still insist on using it, on the whole, and would the essence of what a dojo is change simply by calling it a training hall?

Let us first set the premise that we are talking about good clubs with good instructors. It is a difficult premise to make as one person's idea of good may be very different to another person's. In this case, I would like to state that 'good' means an instructor who has only the best interests of the student at heart and draws upon a balanced and varied wealth of experience when teaching that student.

From the moment we start karate we are controlled by the sensei. They dictate our movements in order to teach us techniques. At first, doing *oi-zuki* is slow and cumbersome. It is hard to imagine that such a movement can be fast or effective, but the control continues and we do as the sensei says.

Over the months the direction from the sensei increases. No longer is it enough to have the correct foot forward, but it is also important to have the knee bent correctly, the weight properly distributed, and no matter how tired one gets, it is also important to maintain one's form. Over the years one's form is completely dictated. Total body control, from the orientation of one's head, to the angle of one's foot, everything is manipulated by one's sensei ... And I think, to a lesser extent, that this never ends ...

What is happening is that the instructor is giving (which is probably a better description than 'teaching') the student a framework of thinking. What I mean by framework of thinking is a set of assumptions and parameters, based on tried-and-tested experience, about what karate is and how it should be done. By initially forcing the student into a strict and stringent way of movement, the student is forced to become more aware of his/her physical actions. This helps them conceptualise body mechanics and increases body awareness ... In essence, through being controlled by the sensei, the student is able to learn how to control their own body.

The same can be seen with the mental aspect of karate. From the moment one walks through the dojo door students are forced to abide by a strict set of rules, which go beyond the simple physical task of putting your left foot forward. No talking in class seems one obvious way of controlling the students, but subtler than that is the use of Japanese language and culture. Introducing a foreign language to the dojo has the effect of setting the time spent training as being different from the normal world. *Osu* is constantly used to communicate a whole wealth of feelings. The word *sensei* has connotations, which set the instructor apart from the rest of the class. And techniques are described using their Japanese term: 'lunge-punch' doesn't quite describe what an *oi-zuki* is.

By forcing people to adhere to the Japanese culture and hierarchical system, it forces them into a strict set of social parameters that they must abide to. By controlling the students' behaviour (what they can and can't do) the student is forced to think about 'life in the dojo' in different terms then what they would in normal life. Simple things like showing politeness to one's seniors, bowing at the correct time, pushing yourself to train harder because your sensei insists you have more to give ... All these ways in which students' behaviour is controlled forces the way they think, and the way they relate to other people, to change.

Life in the dojo can be tough and demanding. Knowing one's place and knowing what is and isn't acceptable behaviour whilst with the sensei can be a daunting task. Over time, however, students can learn the correct manner and abide by it. So, similar to the physical aspect of karate, the mental aspect can be seen as a framework of thinking. From being strictly controlled by one's sensei, students can come to understand their mental actions. From this one has a better ability to develop self-control.

Hopefully, through an initial strict regime of both physical and mental control, karate can provide students with (what every karate advertisement has ever claimed) greater discipline, confidence and coordination. By one's every movement being controlled by the sensei, body coordination is learnt. By the interaction amongst student and sensei being dictated by strict rules, greater discipline can be learnt, culminating in a martial art, which allows the practitioner to have a greater control of mind and body. Therefore, when people ask why it is necessary to use Japanese terminology in the dojo, I think it comes down to the basic need for control. Karate is not merely a set of techniques and rules. That is a simple and rather superficial view of what we do. It is a way of learning and a way of developing a framework of thinking, which better enables us to use our bodies and minds, maximising their efficiency. Without the Japanese language, without the control, I think karate is merely reduced to its physical components, just a series of punches and kicks.

Finally, it is worth noting two points. Firstly, many people, in a knee-jerk reaction, object the idea of themselves being controlled in the dojo. The word control has negative connotations. However, it is possible to see that people, on a regular basis, choose to place themselves in the control of someone else who they judge to be more knowledgeable. Everything from personal fitness trainers at the local gym to weight-watchers' meetings, these people make one easy decision to walk into the gym or town hall and from that moment on they are put under pressure to perform and conform to the wishes of someone else. In essence they are controlled, and they allow this because people realise the need for outside help and guidance and the need to have someone else motivate them.

The second point I would like to make is that my argument regarding the use of Japanese language and culture could be negated by the fact that in Japan, the home of karate, neither the language nor the culture is foreign. But ask any Japanese non-karate-ka and they will tell you that the language and culture that surround karate is equally as foreign to them as it is to us. Most Japanese people don't know how to write *osu* or karate using *kanji* (Japanese pictograms). They usually use *katakana* (the phonetic alphabet reserved for foreign words) and as a result they often think karate is not from Japan. So, even when a person enters a dojo in Tokyo, they still find it somewhat foreign to their normal daily life.

A comparison can be drawn with ballet. Throughout the world, French is used when teaching this artform. Similar to karate, in good ballet schools the teacher can be very strict and controlling. Even in Paris the culture and language surrounding ballet can seem foreign to local Parisians. Native speakers know that *pas de chat* means 'step of the cat', but have no idea what it involves or how difficult it is. *Neko-ashi-dachi* (cat stance) is an obvious comparison within karate. Just because the language spoken may be familiar, it doesn't mean the vocabulary employed is part of daily usage. The language becomes an integral part of the control of the class.

In the West (and also in Westernised Japan), people just aren't used to this way of teaching through total control. But any martial tradition, whether it be the samurai of Japan or the knights of England, has always had a strict physical and mental regime to follow. Then, the need for a comprehensive teaching process was understood for all the reasons I have mentioned above and those of us who practise good Shotokan today can still see the importance of these things as a way of developing good karate.

TEN

Zenkutsu-dachi & the Wobbly Knee

This article was written in 1999, whilst I was still in Japan. I include it now because although there is a great more I would add to a similar article written today, in essence, what I wrote then still holds true.

The first thing that most karate-ka are taught is that stance is the foundation of all karate power. It's more important than upper body strength and targeting, and possibly more important than hip movement, because without a solid foundation, even a strong and accurate technique can be made ineffective. However, one of the most difficult aspects of *Zenkutsu-dachi* is keeping the front knee from shaking and thus weakening the stance. It seems simple enough, to keep the knee still, but when throwing a technique at full speed and power, it often becomes a near-impossible task.

It is important to identify why the knee is so out of control. I have found in many cases that the problem originates in the way we shift our weight from *hanmi* (hips back) to *shomen* (hips square on) and back again. Many people have been taught that the back leg remains straight at all times when twisting the hips and that the pivot action takes place down the centre of gravity. This can be seen in many karate books, where hip movement is shown pivoting along a line that runs from the top of the person's head, right down the centre of the body. However, if you pivot down the centre of the body you will find that the right side hip moves forwards, but the left side hip moves backwards (left leg forward), which obviously pushes the front knee back and forwards when you perform any *hanmi-shomen* movement. This, then, has the effect of shaking your very foundations every time you throw a punch or perform a block.

The way to overcome this problem is to pivot using an axis, which allows you to rotate your hip but at the same time keep your front knee motionless (i.e. pivoting along a line that runs from just inside your left shoulder, down your left side and through your left hip). By pivoting from the left side hip it will enable hip movement without pulling and pushing the knee as the ball-and-socket joint of the hip allows the pelvis to rotate and open up, without affecting the front leg. This means that your whole torso will move backwards in *hanmi* and forwards in *shomen*, creating greater power with increased stability. Not only do you have the twist of the hips, but you also have lateral movement backwards and forwards and all your power and 'weight' can be put behind a technique.

An equally important point in stance stability is knee positioning. Many people don't understand the way in which the knee should point, and I have seen many students with their front knee pushed out to the side – even over their little toe! This is very dangerous to your knee joint, plus it reduces the power of your techniques as the line of power is off to the side and not on target. When making a stance, you should simply start at the beginning. The front foot should be pointing perfectly forward (that is, the outer edge of the foot should be straight, so in actual fact the foot is pointing slightly in) and the back foot should be pointing as much forward as possible (depending on the flexibility of your ankle). Once in this position it is easy to know where the knees should point. The knee is a hinge joint, and as such has only one way to bend; forward. So simply bend the front knee forward, don't push or pull the knee left or right. This is the only way to maintain a triangle of power, that is, whether in *hanmi* or *shomen*, the front and back knee, plus the techniques all point to and converge on the target.

Even when the hip is pulled back into *hanmi*, the back knee should still remain pointing forward. The ball-and-socket joint of the hip allows you to move your pelvis back, and by bending the back knee, the lower leg and knee joint are kept pointing forward, rather than pointing to the side as it does if the back leg is kept straight; the triangle of power is kept. The only part of your stance that moves when performing any technique is your torso and the right thigh, moving forward and back pivoting and moving laterally around the left side hip.

The final part of a correct stance is the 'tucking in' of the tail bone. A lot of people tend to relax the lower back when in front stance and this tends to allow the bum to stick out. One must always, whether in *hanmi* or *shomen*, feel like the tail bone is being 'tucked in' and squeezed forward. This will allow the points of contraction (right hip when in *hanmi* and left hip when in *shomen*) to be maintained. If one does not do this, then it puts excess pressure of the lower back and can cause problems.

SHU-HA-RI – EVOLVING KARATE THOUGHTS

Zenkutsu Dachi *from the front showing the triangle of power. The front and back knee points forward and into target, with the hand pointing to target too, converging to form a traiangle of power.*

Zenkutsu Dachi *from the side – exactly as shown in the photo above..*

SHU-HA-RI – EVOLVING KARATE THOUGHTS

Zenkutsu Dachi – Hanmi, back leg relaxed, hip pulled all the way back, but still allowing both knees to remain pointing forward to maintain triangle of power.

Zenkutsu Dachi — Hanmi with the back leg straight, pivoting from the centre. This pushes the front knee forward and forces the back knee to point out to the side. It also puts excess pressure on the outside of the back foot. Hips can only be brought back to a 45 degree position, unlike when you relax your back leg, allowing the hips to be fully pulled back.

Once these problems have been rectified many people then have the problem of their left knee moving left and right. When performing a technique at full speed and power it is very difficult to stop the pivoting and lateral movement of the hips from pushing and pulling the knee sideways. A common teaching method to prevent this is to have someone hold the knee steady as you practise various techniques. However, the benefits from this are often minimal, as you only become used to the pressure of your partner's grip. In my experience the best way to overcome this problem is to try to mimic your partner's grip on your knee by feeling as if you are slightly pushing and pulling your knee sideways when doing a technique. As your body is moving, it takes active effort to keep other parts of your body still. For example, if you were practising left-hand *kizami zuki*, right-hand *gyaku zuki*, when in *hanmi* (*kizami zuki*) the left knee tends to move inwards as you pull the hips back, and when in *shomen* (*gyaku zuki*) the left knee tends to move outwards with the push of the hips. To prevent this when punching *kizami zuki*, imagine pushing your left knee outwards and this will 'fight' against the knee wanting to move inwards, keeping the knee still.

The same is true for *gyaku zuki*, except this time pull inwards instead. The principle can be used all the time regardless of technique, and if practised slowly at first, then gradually building up speed, it will teach you to be constantly aware of the changes in pressure in your stance, adjust accordingly to maintain stability. With practice it is possible to have a foundation that maximises your stability and at the same time increases your hip power.

I have trained with many great instructors at the JKS Hombu Dojo in Japan. All of them place great emphasis on stance, and the point that is constantly taught is the naturalness of karate. These sensei have trained intensively every day for most of their lives but don't have the same knee and hip injuries that many karate-ka have in Europe: this is because they concentrate on how the *body* works, rather than trying to understand how the *technique* works. Karate is the understanding of the body mechanics and the maximisation of its efficiency. Once the use of the body is mastered it is easy to learn any technique and use it in a natural and safe way. So, the next time your sensei says keep your front knee still, try to understand why this is important, and try to understand your body well enough to know how to do it.

ELEVEN

Shotokan: Best of Both Worlds

This article was written around 2010. It was at a time when I was slowly investigating other ideas within the karate world. Initially Koike Yutaka Sensei had talked about ideas learnt from Steve Ubl Sensei and Paolo Bolaffio Sensei. I would later go on to train with both men and be exposed to a wealth of knowledge that changed my thinking of Shotokan forever.

'What? Shotokan karate isn't that old?'

'It was "invented" this century.'

I was young, I had just started karate, but I remember being almost disappointed when I discovered the Funakoshi Sensei didn't really 'create' Shotokan until his arrival onto mainland Japan in the early part of the twentieth century. I had thought karate was really old, developed over millennia. Here I was practising a recent phenomenon!

Many years have passed since the let-down and I have had the chance to delve a little deeper into where this great art came from. Surprisingly, beyond the historical significance of

SHU-HA-RI – EVOLVING KARATE THOUGHTS

such insight, it has had the effect of fundamentally changing how I view the way I perform Shotokan techniques.

Funakoshi Sensei had two great karate masters as mentors. Asato Sensei was a master of *Shuri-te* and Itosu Sensei was a master of *Naha-te*. From these great men Funakoshi learnt the two ancient karate styles and melded them to form what would become Shotokan. By being more aware of what these two old styles taught, we are more able to understand our own modern style.

Shuri-te is a fast, relaxed style of karate. At no point is there tension within the body and this karate is characterised by wave-like movement of the hips, rotating and moving from side to side. Feet are moved directly to target and back again and breathing is always done at a natural pace. If anyone has seen Shorin-Ryu karate-ka practise the 'paper punch', where they have to use speed rather than brute strength to tear a piece of paper in half, will understand that this style is very much focused on speed to generate power, rather than strength.

Naha-te is the slower, tenser style of karate. With controlled breathing, feet are moved in an arc as you step forward and back in a natural stance. With slower actions, techniques are based on focusing power and strength. Exemplified by *Goju-Ryu* karate, *Naha-te* is the yin to the *Shuri-te* yang.

From these two ancient styles of Okinawan *Te*, Shotokan was developed. Of course, over the years, especially since the death of Funakoshi Sensei and the inauguration of the JKA, Shotokan has developed. But our roots still remain firmly planted within Shuri-te and Naha-te. If we look at Shotokan karate hip movement we rotate from *hanmi* to *shomen*. This is heavily influenced by the wave-like hip motion of *Shuri-te*. At the same time we don't allow our tailbone to stick out.

Not only do we have horizontal rotation (*hanmi-shomen*) but also vertical rotation (*shime* – tucking the tailbone in) and this is from *Naha-te*. When we step forward and back in *Zenkutsu-dachi*, at first we learn the controlled, crescent-shaped movement of feet together, squeeze the inner thigh muscles and then expand out into stance. This is identical to *Naha-te*. As we progress, we go beyond this and move directly from one stance to another. This is identical to *Shuri-te*. The same is true with breathing. When we begin Shotokan we often emphasise our exhalation with a technique; this is the same at *Naha-te*. As we progress through the dan grades this should become more natural, intuitive. No sound should be made: this is identical to *Shuri-te*.

Even within a movement the body can adopt different emphases. Stepping-forward *Oi-zuki* is a good example. The lower body should feel the rooted strength of *Naha-te*. The hips are driven into *shomen-dachi*, maintaining tension within the leading hip by driving the other hip forward whilst squeezing the abdomen to pull the tailbone in. In *Shuri-te* this tension after the moment of *kime* would be considered useless, even inhibitive for subsequent techniques. However, it is an essential part of *Naha-te*. *Naha-te* believes that the tension within the stance is there as preparation for the next move. Maintaining *hanme* or *shomen* is necessary to drive forward or back to deliver the next technique. Stance follows the principles of *Naha-te*.

In conjunction with this, the upper body is following the principles of *Shuri-te*. The upper body is kept completely relaxed as you step forward. We know that tension in the shoulders and chest will only slow down the punching arm and reduced speed means reduced power. At the moment of *kime* the whole body tenses for a split second, but then the upper body is relaxed again, whether you keep your form or not (you can keep your punching arm held out without tensing it). This use of the upper body is following principles of *Shuri-te*.

So, we can see good Shotokan as maintaining internal tension within one's stance whilst maintaining a relaxed posture with the upper body. Bad Shotokan is the opposite. I have seen many karate-ka try to increase their power by tensing their upper body. It is an easy mistake. If we tense our chest and arms we instantly feel stronger – we get that immediate feedback. At the same time, people who fall into this trap often have weak stance with no emphasis on maintaining internal tension. It is almost like they apply the principles of *Naha-te* to their upper body and the principles of *Shuri-te* to their stances ... with disastrous results.

With *Oi-zuki* we see that these two sets of ancient karate principles can apply to a same technique, but we can also see that one set of principles may completely override the other in certain techniques. If we use the kata *Bassai-Dai* as an example we can demonstrate how when we punch *choku-zuki* then block *uchi-uke* twice before stepping forward *shuto-uke*, these techniques are completely following the principles of *Shuri-te*. They are fast and light with only a snap of *kime* with the punch before we use the residual energy to prepare and then block *uchi uke*. The hips are used in a wave-like action and the breathing is natural and understated. However, several moves after we block *tsukami-uke* before kicking *yoko-geri kekomi* and *kiai-ing*. This *tsukami-uke* is pure *naha-te*. There is vertical rotation of the hips, breathing is deliberate and the movements and slow and controlled. Both sets of techniques could not be further from each other in the principles they use to create power.

Shotokan is a hybrid, drawing from the vast amounts of knowledge that were the *Shuri-te* and *Naha-te* systems. For me this is our strength, allowing Shotokan to become the most widespread form of karate in the world. Within the enormous volume of knowledge that we gained from the two systems there is room for people to diversify. Funakoshi Sensei wrote that he thought *Naha-te* was more suited to small, stocky people; whereas *Shuri-te* was more suited to the taller, ganglier practitioner. However, regardless of body type the truth is that Shotokan has something to offer anyone. The Shotokan of Kase Sensei was a world apart from that of Asai Sensei. Kagawa Sensei and Yahara Sensei have different ways of teaching *gyaku zuki*. A course with Kanazawa Sensei or Steve Ubl Snsei may be inspirational to one student and dull as dishwater to another. The point is that it is all Shotokan. And the reason we know that it is all Shotokan is that they apply the principles of *Shuri-te* and *Naha-te* to their karate. More importantly than that, they apply the principles at the right time to the right techniques and the right parts of their body. Understanding where our karate came from will help us to see where we should be aiming for.

TWELVE

Vintage Character vs Modern Technique

This article dates back to 1998. I don't remember having much time to write during my stay in Japan, but obviously I did.

Sensei Bruno Koller 8th dan IJKA (Switzerland), once told me that karate-ka are like cars; that is to say, vintage cars are believed to be superior in many ways to the modern-day production car. However, in reality the average production car can outperform the vintage cars in speed, safety and efficiency. He went on to say that the sensei who founded our great style, although believed to be of such a high quality, were in actual fact much weaker, slower and less effective than the modern day karate-ka. I instantly disagreed with Bruno Sensei in a kind of knee-jerk reaction, but the more I thought about his analogy, the more I came to understand and agree with what he was saying.

Before I continue this article I feel I first must qualify my comments. It goes without saying that the masters of the past were fantastically talented, incredibly strong people, who were responsible for the development of karate from its infancy into the world-wide art it is today. What this article is trying to do is look at the physical development of karate, and as such at times karate will be compared with 'other' sports – although I can assure you that I feel karate is far from a sport.

The evolution of karate is no different from the evolution of other sports. Athletics provides us with a perfect example, as athletes are running faster, throwing further and jumping higher than their counterparts of thirty years ago. In fact, athletes of thirty years ago were similarly doing better than athletes thirty years before that. And although it is possible to say that people are bigger, stronger and healthier as times gone by, it does not account for the constant stream of broken records we see today. What does account for these advancements is the natural evolution of sporting technique. That is, as athletes and coaches become more experienced and develop a greater understanding of body mechanics and technique, athletes are able to use this knowledge to improve performance. If we turn our attention to karate, we are able to see the same thing. Many of us have seen the old JKA Kata tapes and watched with interest to see how kata was done back then, compared with today. I doubt anyone would use these old tapes to improve their technique. It is interesting to note whether the jump in *Unsu* is taken from *Zenkutsu-dachi*, *Kokutsu-dachi* or *kiba-dachi*, but no one would use these tapes to learn how to do the stances. And this is because as the JKA has evolved as an organisation, so too has its technique.

If we take karate's foundation (stance) as an example, it perfectly illustrates this point. I have only been doing karate for thirteen years, but if I were to ask more experienced karate-ka, I am sure they would agree with me in saying that when karate first came to the UK, *hanmi-shomen* hip movement was not given the importance it has today. *Hanmi-shomen* was always taught in *Zenkutsu-dachi*, but never in *kiba-dachi* or *Kokutsu-dachi*. But in recent years, due to increased understanding and evolution of technique, karate in the UK has gone through a revolution with the 'introduction' of *hanmi-shomen* in *kiba-dachi* and *Kokutsu-dachi*. Even *Zenkutsu-dachi* has fundamentally changed with the back leg being relaxed and bent, and the hips being able to be pulled back a lot more than the traditional 45-degree explanation. Plus, within all stances the idea of a triangle of power has been introduced, so that at all times power is concentrated and directed to the target.

As well as stance, hip use in technique has also evolved. The use of hips when performing *yoko geri keage* has fundamentally changed the effectiveness of the kick. I am sure most people first learnt *yoko geri keage* as a simple, fast snapping kick, that was practised by attacking your partner under the armpit! Now we know that if we synchronise the hip snap and the push of the supporting leg, then this produces a much more effective and devastating technique, with the power of *yoko geri kekomi* and the speed of *mae geri*. It is also possible to see that karate has developed into a technically safer 'sport'. How many older karate-ka do you know with knee and hip problems resulting from the way they used to push their knees out over their little toes in *Zenkutsu*, *kiba* and *Kokutsu-dachi*? Over the years this constant unnatural movement and positioning puts excess pressure on joints, resulting in ligament and cartilage problems. Due to the evolution of karate, however, I am sure no instructor in their right mind would still teach such dangerous stances today.

In conclusion, I do not mean to affront the masters of yesteryear – in fact this article is meant as a compliment to them, as every karate-ka in the world today, no matter how high and mighty they may have become, are standing on the shoulders of these old masters. They produced students good enough to continue the development of karate, and if these students had failed to evolve karate, then Shotokan would have simply stagnated and withered away. Without this constant movement forward, we would have very quickly fallen behind. Karate, like anything else, must be constantly on the move, and if the masters of yesteryear are better than the masters of today, then we have been doing something seriously wrong.

THIRTEEN

Ladder to Success

I continue to search for interesting and innovative ways to train smart. This article was born after witnessing the undeniable speed that sports karate athletes generate. 'I want a bit of that!' I thought.

I am amazed and inspired by the speed that international fighters produce in WKF competitions. As a traditionalist I used to dismiss their movement as purely sport karate, lacking the *budo* element that I search for in my own training. Recently, though, I have forced myself to see past the sometimes superficiality of their movement and tried to see what I can learn, as a traditionalist, from the sport of WKF karate. After numerous conversations with coaches of national teams I have learnt that plyometric exercises and agility ladders are often used to increase the speed of these dynamic fighters.

First coined in 1975 by the American track and field coach Fred Wilt, plyometric exercises revolutionised athletics, although it seems that sport karate took its time adopting the principles. Plyometric training is the idea of exercising the muscle whilst it is loaded. The result is increased explosive power from the muscle or muscle group that is exercised. A simple example of plyometrics would be standing in *shizentai* and then jumping forward into a squat, before jumping back into the *shizentai* position. The idea is that when you jump forward into the squatted position you load your leg muscles before pushing back into *shizentai*, thus producing greater results than, say, if you did simple slow lunges into a deep *Zenkutsu-dachi* from *shizentai*.

The reasoning and science behind these exercises can be and should be explained by a source of greater knowledge than myself and this article and further research can easily be done by googling it. I simple would like to convey a few ideas that I know work through personal experience.

EXERCISE NO. 1. From a deep lunge, keep the back straight and your height constant as you switch quickly, simultaneously pulling the front leg back and the back leg forward. Forcing your quads to work under pressure, this exercise increases the explosive nature of your muscles and can help develop fast, dynamic movements from one stance to another.

EXERCISE NO. 2. Standing on your bent left leg (with your right foot tucked behind your left knee) punch *choku-zuki* with your right hand. From this position, maintain the same height and drive forward 45-degree changing leg and as you land punch *choku-zuki* with the left hand. The idea is to maintain the same height throughout and drive off the supporting leg whilst it is loaded.

Exercise No. 3. For the final exercise start in *Kokutsu-dachi*, blocking *shuto-uke*. From this position, maintain the same height and drive the back leg forward into *Zenkutsu-dachi* and punch *oi-zuki* with the leading hand. From this position drive the front leg back into *Kokutsu-dachi*, blocking *shuto-uke*. The idea is not to move forward or back, but to maintain the same position. You must try not to jump up as you are changing stance. By maintaining the same height as you move from *Kokutsu-dachi* to *Zenkutsu-dachi* and vice versa, you must keep the particular leg that you are working loaded at all times.

Hopefully with these three exercises it is possible to see how simple it is to take a plyometric exercise and gradually apply it to traditional karate training. With the final exercise, if done correctly, you are only working one leg throughout the routine and very quickly you should feel 'the burn'. This is far more productive than marching up and down the dojo doing *oi-zuki* and *shuto-uke*, plus you are developing explosive power in your muscles.

The second idea I have stolen from WKF fighters is the agility or speed ladder. Tennis coaches etc have been using these for years to increase the foot speed of their athletes and when I started using one I felt the immediate effects. Five minutes of ladder drills and my legs were aching all day! I quickly grew accustomed to the training and now incorporate it into my regular workout.

An agility ladder can be bought at many sports shops or easily online. It is simply a flat plastic ladder that can be laid on the ground. With this simple piece of kit you can practise in many ways. However, for a karate club, it is not essential. For example, many dojo train in sports halls where there are a variety of markings on the floor that can be used. Also, simply taking off belts and laying them on the floor to make a ladder pattern works very well. The following set of exercises start with the agility ladder and then move onto more karate exercises whilst maintaining the same focus.

EXERCISE NO. 4. Starting at the beginning of the ladder, move as quick as you can your right then left foot into each of the squares. Once at the end, move back to the beginning and do the same, but with your body facing sideways; again once completed move to the beginning and start from the side. If to the left of the ladder, move your right, then left foot into the first square. Then step to the right of the second square. Follow this with your left then right foot into the second square before stepping to the right left of the third square. Repeat this movement so you are zig-zagging along the ladder as fast as you can.

There are many foot combinations you can create with the ladder, but essentially you are trying to increase the speed of your foot movement by upping the speed of your repetitions. Once these patterns have been mastered, try adding a competitive edge with a partner trying to catch the person in front, giving the lead person decreasingly shorter head starts.

EXERCISE NO. 5. Stand with a partner with your hands on each other's shoulders. Start with one person trying to stand on the toes of the other. The 'defender' must stay within range, whilst trying to avoid being trodden on. Once both sides have developed a certain amount of speed, they can both defend and attack at the same time. The object of this exercise to adapt the speed gained with the ladder into a more dynamic and undetermined way.

Exercise No. 6. The last exercise is practising tag-kumite. From a normal *jiyu kamae* position each person must score against their partner by touching them on the inner thigh. Taking the danger of *jiyu* kumite away, by limiting the attacks to simple slaps on the leg, it enables the practitioner to focus on foot speed. This can be taken a step further and instead of using hands to touch the inner thigh, you can use the foot with light, fast *mawashi-geri*. This, again, forces the practitioner to quickly move in and out of range and develop fast foot work.

Again, I hope that you can see that with these three simple exercises it is possible to take the training methods of sport karate and apply them to traditional karate.

Over the last number of years I have learnt that we cannot become narrow-minded in our development. Often working outside of the comfort zone can only be beneficial. My instructor, Kagawa Sensei, as big and as strong as he is, is always insistent that physical strength isn't power: speed is power. Therefore, any type of training that can increase speed and explosive power, no matter how contemporary, can only help our karate development. I have heard many fellow karate-ka complain that WKF fighters may move fast, but lack that vital *kime* at the end of their technique and therefore dismiss WKF karate as weak. I believe they miss the point. Traditional karate-ka know how to make *kime*. And it follows that if we develop the dynamic movements of WKF karate and add *kime* at the end of our technique, our karate must develop.

FOURTEEN

Kata – The Algebra of Karate

This article was written as a result of a trip I made to the UK and Ireland with Yasuhisa Inada. In April 2002 we toured the British Isles and taught at various dojos, the first of which was John Cheetham's –the editor of Shotokan Karate Magazine. During post-training drinks this topic was discussed, and I decided to produce an article.

I often think I have completely changed my view of karate and all the nerdy stuff that surrounds it, but reading the article again now, sixteen years later, I realise that the principles I thought important then still dominates much of what I teach today.

Travelling around various dojos, teaching and training, and reading magazines such as *SKM*, I have often heard the argument that kata is a waste of time, meaningless and at very best, just a way to pass *kyu* and dan tests. The critics then usually continue with an attack on kata *bunkai*, claiming it's contrived and impractical. On the opposite side of the spectrum, though, I have also heard the arguments that kata is the true root of karate and that kata *bunkai* holds its true meaning.

I thought I would jump head first into the old debate and give my opinion (for what it's worth). Personally, I think kata has one overwhelming use, and that is to teach one how to use one's body. Kata *bunkai* on the other hand has other benefits, which will be discussed later. For now, let us just concentrate on kata as a set of movements.

The people who complain about the impracticality of kata and claim that the best way to become a strong fighter, in whatever context, is to practise fighting (kumite), always remind me of those naughty kids at the back of the class who say, 'Hey sir, why do we have to learn algebra? I'll never use this stuff when I leave school!' (I used to be a teacher). The thing is, those types of students are completely missing the point. Algebra provides a framework of thinking for the brain that allows it to work out problems logically so that when the child grows up and leaves school, it is much better equipped to deal with daily anxieties such as tax returns, budgeting and alimony payments, than a person who can't approach things in a logical manner.

I'm sure there are those people who say, 'I went to the University of Life and it never did me any harm,' which may be quite true, but the point is this, the better equipped you are for life, the better chance you have to succeed.

So, what's this got to do with karate? Well, in the same way algebra provides a logical framework of thinking for our minds, kata provides us with a logical framework of thinking for our bodies. Going from *Heian Shodan* to *Unsu*, kata provides us with a step-by-step method of learning how to use the body to its maximum efficiency. By practising the same movements repeatedly, we can learn the limitations, distancing and mechanics of our body, resulting in greater efficiency.

With this in mind, I feel that the purpose behind kata is the development of one's understanding of one's body. Many people claim that kata is contrived, especially the *Heian* katas, with their blocks moving forward into the attack and having no immediate counter-attack. And in many ways algebra is contrived too – but what it is doing is starting from a basic point, giving the student a foundation to build on, and then progressing onto advanced mechanics. Kata is the same, starting with easily understandable techniques, then progressing onto advanced body mechanics.

Critics then go on to say that kata training will never be as effective as kumite training, but again, I feel they are missing the point. Referring back to our algebra metaphor, people claim that the 'school of rough knocks' can't be beaten, and that there is nothing wrong with learning the 'hard way'. However, how can we expect the majority of children to survive this? Some will, but most won't. The same is true with karate-ka. To increase their odds of success we must start with a good foundation and then give them an opportunity to build on it. That foundation is kata. They can learn body mechanics, body-timing, and *kime*, in conjunction with basic kumite, and then when they have a fair understanding of it, they can apply it for 'real' in *jiyu*-kumite.

If we look at kata in this way, arguments such as what is the true application of the first *gedan barai* in *Heian Shodan*, become moot. The true meaning is to teach the student vital body mechanics: how to drop one's weight, pivot on the heel, use the back leg to thrust the body forward, time the hips to land in *hanmi* with one's stance and ultimately how to execute a decent *gedan barai*. I am not saying that the application of kata is pointless, far from it. However, before I go any further, I feel it's important to point out that as it stands now it is probably impossible to determine the original meaning of every move of every kata.

Since Funakoshi Sensei brought the kata to mainland Japan, karate has changed considerably. Consequently, although some moves remain the same, some moves have changed beyond recognition. I want to tell a story that will demonstrate this point perfectly (and before anybody starts to denounce me as a heretic, I got this information directly from Asai Sensei.)

A very long time ago the kata *Nijushiho* was practised with two *fumi-komi geri*, (stamping kicks) as opposed to the now customary two *yoko geri kekomi*. This part of the kata (*Nijushiho*) would originally have been from *kiba dachi*; *tsukame-uke*, (catching block) then *fumi-komi* (stamping kick) followed by *gyaku zuki* (reverse punch) to the side – you can see this interpretation on the old JKA movie film from around 1955/56 when a senior instructor demonstrates *Nijushiho*. About fifty-five years or so ago this was changed to the now common practice of using *yoko-geri kekomi*. Why? And, by whom? Well about that time Asai Sensei and Okazaki Sensei trained on the JKA instructors' course. During training they thought it would be a good idea to introduce *yoko geri kekomi* into the kata because they were young, supple, could easily do it and (I quote directly) 'It looked cool.' A couple of years later Asai Sensei was the first person to do this new version in a competition. No one seemed to complain – in fact the opposite is true. People were very impressed, he won the competition that year (JKA All Japan) and the kata was changed forever.

What does this show us? Firstly, this is one example of karate kata being changed drastically from the original. Therefore, the original *bunkai* was lost. We really have no idea how many other examples of this type we could find. Secondly, changes were made for reasons that don't exactly fit the image of 'Past karate masters passing down their legacy through the practice of kata.' In truth, kata in many Japanese Shotokan dojo has been seen merely as a way to teach how to maximise the efficiency of our body. Before Asai Sensei introduced the *kekomi* into *Nijushiho*, no such kick was practised in Shotokan kata. Once Asai Sensei did it, it was widely accepted. If this addition merely had the benefit of 'looking cool', I'm sure it wouldn't have gained such acceptance. So, when a student asks, 'What is the application of *yoko geri ke-komi* in *Nijushiho*?' you should answer, 'The application is to develop strong hips, leading to a strong *yoko-geri kekomi*.'

I mentioned before, I do feel kata *bunkai* has an important place in karate. Let's use the analogy of poetry. If one reads a poem, sometimes the meanings are obvious, sometimes more obscure. One can academicise it by claiming the author, when writing the poem, meant this, that or the other, with a particular construction of words. In truth, one can only claim to understand what that particular poem means to oneself, not to anyone else. Of course one can go to university, study with great professors who give us a foundation of knowledge and insight, but ultimately, after all one's studies, one must decide what the poetry means to oneself. The same is true with kata. As demonstrated earlier, kata has changed, karate has developed and so it is often impossible to understand the original meaning of every move of every kata. But what one can do is teach, demonstrate and practise what the kata means to oneself (obviously only after many years of training and of building a solid foundation).

Let's take the first move of the first kata as an example.

Yoi position – Scott Langley and Yasuhisa Inada. The first position on Heian Shodan

Gedan barai to the left in *Heian Shodan* is usually described as blocking an opponent who is executing a *mae geri* from one's left-hand side. This interpretation is fine, although it does have a few problems regarding distancing (i.e. why does one step into the attack, rather than back). However, there are other interpretations. For example, from *shizentai*, one must drop one's weight, turn the hips towards the target and prepare for *gedan barai* by bringing the left hand to the side of the right ear and the right hand out as the guide arm.

But with a little imagination (no more than is needed for the standard *mae geri* interpretation) let's imagine our opponent attacking with a left-hand *jodan gyaku zuki*. As the opponent comes in, one drops one's weight, and uses the left (preparation) hand to block the punch, with *nagashi uke*. We

Block the jodan punch with nagashi uke whilst simultaneously attacking with gyaku zuki.

Continue the attack by stepping forward with gedan barai uchi.

can also use the power of the hip preparation (twist) to deliver a *chudan gyaku zuki* to the attacker (all from *shizentai*). From this position we can then step forward and use the *gedan barai*, not as a block, but as an attack to the groin (*gedan uchi*). With this simple example it is possible to see that with even the simplest of techniques, *kata bunkai* can be experimented with and adapted, allowing one's karate to evolve and grow.

In conclusion, my point is this: like everything, karate (and kata) has many levels. If we return to algebra, the problems we learn at school are very basic; they are foundations. However, talk to a professor of maths, and they will talk about patterns, the beauty, in fact the poetry of maths. Karate is the same.

The practice of kata and *kata bunkai* are intrinsically joined, but it's important not to over-academicise kata. A *gedan barai* is a *gedan barai*. One practises it in kata to become good at doing *gedan barai*. Only when this is understood and mastered can we move onto the next level, finding the poetry that is at the heart of every kata.

FIFTEEN

The Straightening of Karate

This was published in 2011. Yutaka Koike had moved to Ireland and was teaching full time at my dojo. Although a JKS instructor, he had studied extensively with Paolo Bolaffio in Italy and brought to the Hombu Dojo and my practice different aspects of what karate could be. It results in this article and, I believe, represents the beginning of me being comfortable with my own karate developments. Maybe it also represents the start of the end with my relationship with Japan.

Shotokan karate is often known for and characterised by its straight, dynamic, direct techniques. But is that all Shotokan has to offer? Is this how it has always been? I hope, in this article, to explore the rounder, more circular aspects of our style and maybe give a few ideas about how we can increase, or at least revisit, the depth and breadth of our style.

Let me start with the premise that I believe Shotokan

karate has been straightened over the years. What I mean by this is that techniques that were once round and circular have been made more linear and, therefore, externally dynamic. There are a number of reasons for this. The first and foremost, I believe, is competition. It is almost impossible to control a circular technique. Therefore, the straight techniques (*gyaku zuki*, *kizami zuki* etc) are almost exclusively used. This is for a number of reasons. To use *sundome* or control, we must be able to focus our technique without making contact. Control is used for a variety of reasons, not merely to protect one's opponent, but also to understand how to create the snap of one's technique – ultimately making one's technique more destructive when hitting an opponent. These techniques also have the advantage of having external *kime* – that is spectators (judges, referees and examiners) can see their power. We can see in competitions, gradings and in the dojo, techniques that are obviously rounded being done in the straight manner. Ask any group of experienced karate-ka (and believe me, I have) to do *kagi zuki*, the course of their fists will go from *hikite* to the finished position in an almost direct line. Ask them to do *shuto* or *haito uchi* and a similar thing will happen. If we look at how people perform kata, the same phenomenon happens. In Heian Yondan the sequence before the first *kiai* is often performed as dynamic, sharp, straight techniques, when in actual fact the *shuto uchi*, *osae uke* and *tate uraken* are all circular. In more advanced kata the same has happened. How many people perform the *haito uchi* in *Unsu* in a circular fashion? (YouTube 'Nakayama Unsu' to see how Nakayama Sensei did it!)

Of course, this emphasis is completely understandable. It would be impossible to make external *kime* and finish one's technique in a precise manner (two factors that are important when been judged or examined) if techniques are done in a circular fashion. To perform such precise, dynamic movements takes great body control, which, after all, is what we are trying to achieve through karate. But does that mean we should neglect this circular aspect of Shotokan?

I believe it shouldn't be neglected. In fact, we should take steps to make our karate as complete and comprehensive as possible. What should we be doing? First, we have seen reasons why this aspect of our *budo* has been somewhat avoided. However, we must also investigate the innate difficulties of practising such *waza*.

With a technique such as *Haito Uchi*, it is possible to practise it slowly to target (your partner's temple, for example); it is possible to practise the technique with speed and power, but it isn't possible to practise both precision and speed at the same time. If we performed *Haito Uchi* speed and power to target, it would be impossible to control. The same is true with so many of these techniques. Therefore, over the years, the way we do them has changed.

What can we do to rectify this problem? Simple! Just accept that the above it true. Practise slowly with one's partner, making sure the course and targeting is correct and also practise full speed with one's partner, but miss, therefore preventing you from having to artificially snap or control your technique. In the case of *Haito Uchi*, just let your technique flow past the target; don't expect or try to make an artificial '*kime*' at the point where you would normally hit your partner. Of course, the final way to practise is by using a focus pad. Not all dojos have these, of course, but they are a great way to really see how effective these techniques actually are. If you are hitting a pad, realise that the way to make power is simply to relax through the target. Don't tense or try to make *kime* as we would with straight technique – but in my experience, even with seasoned karate-ka, after years of making straight *kime* with every technique, making power with a rounded technique often proves problematic![1]

Although I have already mentioned a few techniques in the above, I would like to continue to highlight a few more that I feel can really be made more effective in most people's karate with the correct training.

I have already mentioned *Shuto* and *Haito Uchi*, so I would like to start with *Kagi Zuki*. It appears in *Heian Godan*, of course, and is a common punch throughout Shotokan. Unfortunately, I feel it is completely misunderstood. With *Kagi Zuki* the first is coming in a circular course from the hip as the shoulder relaxes and the body shifts its weight around the target. It is a very close-quarter technique and the punch should never overreach to hit the target. Done correctly it can deliver a devastating amount of heavy *kime*.

Kagi zuki – Front Cover of Shotokan Karate Magazine Issue No. 109.

The way we move when performing any of these

---

1. I feel compelled at this point to insert a footnote mentioning that I have often seen people do the inverse – that is, try to make this hard heavy *kime* with straight techniques. Punching or (snap-) kicking focus pads should not produce any visible effect as the snap should occur several centimetres into the pad. But people like to see results and end up pushing into the pad so the partner feels the technique – or at the very least staggers back! This is a waste of a good snapping technique.

techniques is very important. Shotokan is characterised by Kendo's *Yori-ashi*, *Yose-ashi* etc, but these are generally only useful for straight techniques. Circular, *tai-sabaki* movements are essential and with the case of *Kagi-Zuki* one must not move towards, but around and besides the target – think Japanese straight-blade, Kenjitsu movements versus the Chinese curved-blade, Kung-fu movements. If we compare how often we practise moving in and out of range in a linear fashion to this circular *tai-sabaki* movement, we can see how Shotokan has favoured straight, competition-type karate.

We often see the same straightening of *waza* in *Mawashi Uke* and *Mawashi Uchi*, which are (albeit in slightly different ways) at the end of the kata *Nijushiho* and *Unsu*. It has been one of my pet hates for years, seeing people perform these flowing blocks and strikes in a stiff straight way. For example, at the end of *Nijushiho* karate-ka will block with their right hand, bringing it down to their right hip, whilst the left hand circles to the left shoulder – so far so good-ish. They will then step forward and perform *Mawashi-Uchi* in a straight, pushing manner. The same can be seen in *Unsu*. This shouldn't be! The whole technique should be a circular, flowing, continuous action whereby the block seamlessly leads to the strike in an unbroken manner. Today, this graceful *waza* is often executed rigidly with a bit of artificial *kime* added at the end for good measure.

YouTube Nakayama Sensei and you will undoubtedly find footage of him demonstrating *Mawashi Zuki*. Of course, this technique does not appear in any Shotokan kata. However, *Age Zuki* does and I guess if *Mawashi Zuki* did exist in kata it would be straightened similar to how *Age Zuki* has been in *Enpi*. Nakayama Sensei placed importance in *Mawashi Zuki*, I think we should too! I once had a conversation with Asai

Sensei about the aim of karate and *Budo*. He talked about how learning karate helps you do the things that everyone else does, but better. The classic bar-brawl swing punch was mentioned. People throw them because they are effective at producing power. By doing karate, we should be able to highlight and refine that power, not dismiss it at useless.

Mikazuki Geri and *Ura Mikazuki Geri* are also in need of a technical 'check-up'. Most people perform *Mikazuki Geri* in kata like *Heian Godan* with the main objective of slapping the underneath of their right foot to their outstretched left hand. In reality, this has no meaning. I can understand its purpose, but we must also understand the usefulness of this effective kick. Try bringing your leg out to the side and using your inner thigh muscles to drive the leg across to target (of course keeping your knee slightly bent on impact to protect the knee). There is no need to snap back, just allow all the power to go into the target and if you use the knuckle of your ankle as the impact point, this kick is fast and powerful. The same is true with *Ura Mikazuki Geri*. Although not present in any Shotokan kata, it is there in others (*Rantai*, for example) and is used extensively in *Kyokushin Karate*. With practice it can be used to great effect at close-quarter sparring and is extremely powerful.

The final technique I would like to look at is *Mawashi Geri*. In Shotokan, over the years, we have opted for the snapping, fast style of *Mawashi Geri*, which uses the ball of the foot as its impact point. However, if we look at how *Kyokushin* karate do *Mawashi Geri* it is very different. Using their shin, they swing their legs like powerful clubs, heavily impacting their opponents. I believe there is a place for such techniques within Shotokan. It is different, the distance and timing change, but this type of kick is undeniably effective.

Ura Mikazuki Geri

One thing to note with all the techniques mentioned above is that with rounded techniques (as mentioned before) you are not driving your weight forward in a straight line. This, of course, makes their range shorter (medium- to short-range distance). It also means that the need to maintain *Seichusen* (correct centre line) is less important. When performing *Haito Uchi*, *Mawashi Geri* or even *Kagi Zuki*, going off line dramatically helps the technique produce power. Even leaning in, dropping weight down further increases the effectiveness of the *waza*. This, of course, often feels completely alien to Shotokan karate-ka, were the *Seichusen* is sacred!

So far, I have predominantly been talking about circular attacks; however, circular blocks are also a vital part of

Shotokan karate. If we take the kata *Chinte* as an example, there are a huge variety of *waza* that simply don't fit into these linear, *kime*-inducing movements. Near the start of the kata, just after the first *kiai*, there is a sequence, which starts with *Ude Barai*, *Tetsui Uchi* and continues through to double *Uchi Uke*. I have seen this whole set being done stiffly, making *kime* at each 'finish point' and I can't help think that something has been lost when the kata is performed that way.

Instead, try swinging your right fist (and arm) from shoulder height, arcing down to block with the inner forearm. Then, without making '*kime*', allow the movement to continue round and you stand up and perform *Tetsui Uchi* in a similar encircling way. This type of movement is difficult but made more so by the desire to stop dead – to make *kime* – at the perceived end of the block/attack. If you try to artificially add *kime*, it will stiffen and straighten the movement. But doing it correctly/circularly may produce a far less aesthetically (superficially) pleasing performance ... It's the price you have to pay.

The following circular blocks are identical to the previous sequence in how they should be approached. Think of the swirling, graceful movements of *Aikido*. Think of the numerous possible *bunkai* that could apply to such movements. Think of how these blocks would work when adding *tai-sabaki* and maybe *Chinte* will no longer be considered a ladies' kata.

In conclusion, I feel that this straightening of Shotokan has its merits. It has produced a long- to medium-range style of fighting and it is safe in so many ways. Techniques can be controlled allowing for semi-contact kumite, but this also gives us the added benefit of understanding snap *kime*, which can be devastating when used correctly. Also, straight techniques are safer for us. If we kick *Mawashi Geri* and miss our target, we still have the ability to land in a stable *kamae* and continue fighting, whereas if we kick *Mawashi Geri* in this rounded, *Kyokushin* karate style and miss, then we may end up landing in a very vulnerable *kamae* – the same can be said for all such circular techniques. That said, I do believe that these circular techniques are often under-practised and misunderstood within Shotokan. The fourth move of *Heian Shodan* is circular in nature – so right from the start Shotokan is trying to be complete. Kata is littered with techniques that only work when performed in a circular fashion, whose effectiveness is reduced when performed straight, with external, snapping *kime*.

When I lived in Japan, on my way home from the train station I would pass a full-time *Kyokushin* karate dojo. Almost every time I passed there would be karate-ka doing partner work in two variety of ways. Either they would be with their partner slowly doing *Jiyu Kumite*, using *Mawashi Zuki*, *Mawashi Geri*, *Ura Mikazuki Geri* etc in a slow, relaxed manner. They would slowly continue and if any technique hit its target, it was slow enough to not cause damage. Or they had the focus pads out and whilst one partner held it, the other would punch, kick and strike the pad with devastating effect.

I believe Shotokan is the most comprehensive style of karate out there. But this is only true if we practise all aspects of our style. Of course, individuals will favour one aspect over the other, but if one aspect is completely abandoned, for whatever reason, then Shotokan can only suffer as a result.

SIXTEEN

Take a Deep Breath

By the end of 2012, when this next article was written, I had trained with Steve Ubl on a number of occasions. He revolutionised the way I thought about karate and this article was born from watching him very carefully on one occasion when he taught in Scotland. His breathing was deliberate, but natural, and it led to a long conversation about the matter.

'Breathe in as you prepare – breathe out when you execute the technique' ... I can still remember my original instructor getting me to focus on this primitive, intrinsic concept of breathing. As a beginner I found, as I am sure most of the readers did, it difficult to coordinate and develop control over one's breathing whilst training. However, over the years, this (like many other aspects of karate) became engrained – second nature – to the point where I didn't really think about it anymore. Isn't that the point of karate? Practise something until it become a natural movement?

Recently I have been revaluing a few ideas. There are lots

of things that I did as a beginner that I no longer do now. They were very basic, rudimentary principles that remain important, but have often been superseded by more intricate or sophisticated principles. A good example is when I first learnt *Kihon*, I learnt *unsoku* (foot movement). When moving forward or backward in *Zenkutsu-dachi*, I was instructed to bring my feet together at the halfway point. Now, of course, I just move directly, in a straight line. Whilst still using my inner thigh muscles to maintain tension within my stance that the basic lessons taught me, I have made the movement more efficient. I would not have been able to do this if I hadn't practised the basic position, and once it has been internalised, I moved on. So why isn't breathing any different? What are the more advanced methods that I should be using?

At this point, it may be worth pointing out that most of what I am going to highlight in this article, the vast majority of senior karate-ka will do naturally, but this may be done mindlessly – that is without conscious thought. I believe that we must always be able to understand and fully control our actions and movements in order to master them. Therefore, doing something naturally, without previous thought or control, limits one's ability to progress. Furthermore, some people may not be doing what I am about to focus on. These people need to be taught it … It is very difficult to teach something you have never actually spent any time thinking about. Furthermore, the people who are not doing this need a simple way to produce relaxed, fluid movements. I teach professionally all over the world and wherever I go I can see this stiff and rigid karate. Having the tools to prevent this is vital to improve your karate.

Let us start with the basic *gyaku zuki* from a stationary *Zenkutsu-dachi*; try it and think about when you breathe in and when do you start your exhale. Most people I have asked this question to breathe in and then start the exhale as they start the punch. But try this: slowly start an out breath just before the punch, then allow this to smoothly lead to a fast exhalation as you punch *gyaku zuki*. I hope, if you try it, you will immediately see a more fluid start to your punch. The act of starting your out breath before your technique primes your body for action, producing a natural, relaxed start of the technique. Whereas breathing in then starting your punch as you start to breathe out results in a slight tension, which inhibits the start of the technique, reducing fluidity.

Next, try stepping forward *gedan barai* from *shizentai*. Most people I have asked say they breathe in as they prepare and then out as they execute the block. But if we think about the block preparation it is all about contracting the chest, pulling the blocking arm up and in … not really conducive to breathing in! Try this: preface your movement again with the start of the out breath, then as you prepare exhale rapidly and continue to do so as you make the block. Of course, the breath will follow the tempo of the movement and you shouldn't try to rapidly breathe out for the entire movement. Instead allow the movement to dictate tempo, but make sure you never stop the out breath and this will produce a smoother, faster technique.

Of course, with the previous two examples, the techniques naturally produce an out breath, but this isn't always the case. For example, with *soto uke*, whether stepping forward from *shizentai* or making a full step from *Zenkutsu-dachi*, the expansion of the chest during preparation naturally lends itself to the basic method of inhalation on preparation and exhalation on the execution of the block … The point being, what I have described above are simply further tools that can be used on a case-by-case basis when training.

The next exercise I would like you to try is punching *choku zuki* ten times in fast succession. Not too rapidly that you don't breathe at all. Not too slowly that it is possible to breathe in completely between each punch. Some people will do this naturally, others won't. However, what you should be aiming for is; breathe out whilst punching, then the very act of making *kime* and relaxing afterwards makes you draw breath in. *Kime* should create an instant of total body tension, but instantly you relax, releasing the abdomen, which should allow air back into your lungs, replenishing some of the air you used to punch. The result is that you should be able to punch ten times and not feel out of breath afterwards, but yet you haven't consciously thought about taking an in breath.

Until now, we have talked about how to make *kime* on an out breath – but should this always be the case? How about making *kime* in an in breath? This may seem strange but if we allow our techniques to somewhat dictate our breath it becomes logical. Try making a short-range *yoko empi*, not one where you are sliding into *kida-dachi*, but close quarter, maybe to a target standing next to you. From a *Yoi*, relaxed, position it feels so natural to make a sharp in breath as you execute the technique. Or how about *nagashi uke*? We use it so much not only in kumite, but also kata. To make an in breath as you draw your opponent's attack towards and then past you, then to exhale on the counter helps to produce a more fluid, relaxed and effective technique.

Mastering different breathing methods is only half the story. Like karate, not only must we learn techniques, we must also train our body physically to be able to do them. Breathing is no different. Recently, I climbed along to Inca Trail in Peru, eventually making it to Machu Picchu. I was above 3500 m for a week, reaching a height of 4200 m on one peak. I suffer badly from altitude sickness and it took considerable effort to suck in enough oxygen in every breath to keep my body (and mind!) from going. I found myself focusing entirely on my diaphragm, drawing it down to breathe from the *tanden*. It worked and I made it. But it was an important lesson for me to strengthen my respiratory muscles. Since my return I have taken occasionally to training in a gas mask – you may laugh, but it helps. The gas mask restricts the speed at which breath can be sucked in so that every gulp of air takes great effort. If you have one lying around at the back of your air-raid shelter, try doing a kata or some *kihon* at speed to see the instant effects it has … over time it gets easier as your diaphragm becomes stronger.

In conclusion, once you have these concepts in mind, it is possible to apply the breathing methods and training to combinations. Many people rush combinations, others produce jerky, stilted movements. However, I believe that if you breathe correctly, master the different ways to breathe and then apply them naturally in a case-by-case manner, then your karate can become much more fluid, produce a faster more relaxed start, become less stiff and tense and ultimately produce far more effective and powerful techniques.

SEVENTEEN

Shapeless Karate

The seminar mentioned in the following article was the last time I taught for the JKS. I was suspended a week later and forced to leave the month after. I was happy that that was the last class I ever taught for the JKS. It represented my journey up until then. The article was written during a month of turmoil as I faced disciplinary action from the Hombu Dojo – I was glad to have something to focus on and I am glad to publish it again here.

I recently taught at the rather pleasantly packed JKS England Christmas Course. After a bit of 'dynamic on-the-spot basics', SKM's very own Claire Worth sidled up beside me and said, 'Great class – how about an article on Shapeless Karate?' So here it is!

In recent years I have found myself increasing saying 'stop making shapes'. On the same course as mentioned above there was a rather large dan examination – nearly 70 per cent regrettably failed, the main reason being they were merely making shapes, not actually doing karate. But this is more than just a throwaway comment. 'Making shapes,' I believe, is at the core of most people's problems with karate.

Please search YouTube for Tetsuhiko Asai Sensei and Junior Lefevre Sensei performing Heian Nidan. The two clips are easy to find. http://www.youtube.com/watch?v=DqGamx5dyc8

The first clip is of Tetsuhiko Asai Sensei performing *Heian Nidan*; the second is of Junior Lefevre Sensei doing the same. Obviously, there is an age difference between these two sensei, but even taking this into account, is it possible to decide who is best? Of course, in a competition context, Junior Sensei is the best. One of the greatest competitors ever to grace the WKF arena, he is still in great demand as a coach throughout the world and is a truly great athlete. Asai Sensei, on the other hand, was a pioneer and innovator of karate. Chief Instructor of the JKA and then founder of the JKS, he is arguably one of the most influential karate-ka of the last century. Externally, Junior Sensei moves faster, more dynamically. So, from the spectators' point of view Junior Sensei is the best. However, on many occasional I had the 'pleasure' of training, demonstrating and being hit by Asai Sensei. It was like being hit by a white-hot blade. The technique would cut through you and linger well after the moment. Asai Sensei's technique had an element that went well beyond the superficial. I have never had the pleasure of training with Junior Sensei, so I would not like to comment on his karate, other than to say that he moves exceptionally well and has reached the pinnacle of competition karate: but therein lies the problem. When karate is accessed by spectators (albeit trained judges and referees), karate will inevitably migrate into making shapes.

At this juncture I would like to point out that I don't wish this article to deteriorate into a messy discourse about competition vs traditional karate. Firstly, within Shotokan, I don't believe there is anything we can truly call 'traditional' and, secondly I believe that WKF and competition karate is often the vanguard of training methods within our style.

So let me describe exactly what I do mean. On the course mentioned above, I will describe what I taught and explain my rationale behind each of the three exercises, although all we really did was *gedan barai* then *choku zuki* from *shizentai*.

EXERCISE 1. Start in *shizentai* and block *gedan barai* at a 45-degree angle. Then, in the same direction, punch *choku zuki*, although the use of the hips resembles *gyaku zuki*. From this point, repeat the simple combination in the opposite 45-degree angle. Whilst performing these two simple techniques, the focus point should be the use of the hips and shoulders. The techniques should be a manifestation of the internal movement, rather than the sole focus of the training. Therefore, when preparing for *gedan barai*, make sure the hip is rotated to the maximum in the direction of the block (so if you are about to block with the left hand, ensure the right hip is rotated forward, contracting the left hip). At the same time, engage your pectoral muscles, squeezing the shoulders forward in preparation for the block. These points of contraction, by their very nature, are fleeting and momentary. As soon as maximum contraction is reached, the hips and shoulders are released to create the snap of the block. Then, at the moment of *kime* with the block, the right hip and shoulder are contracted back with the *hikite*. This point of contraction is, again, fleeting before releasing it for the punch.

EXERCISE 2. Superficially, the techniques are starting to change, but the internal body mechanics remain the same. Instead of focusing heavily on the preparation of the *gedan barai*, whip the blocking arm from the previous punching position directly into the block. If the arm is relaxed (like any whip) and the movement is started from one's centre, the arm should follow a general *gedan bari* preparation position. However, the fleeting contraction points, as mentioned above, have been further internalised. The resulting action should be a fluid, dynamic block, followed by a standard punch.

EXERCISE 3. The final exercise is taking the principle of shapeless karate even further. Without relying on *hikite*, which tends to punctuate and stylise one's karate, just try to perform the same fleeting internal contractions and expansions and allow these movement from the centre to create external power. Muscle memory will probably insist that you make the shapes of karate, forcing the blocking hand up towards the shoulder in preparation for the block, or the punching hand to the hip as you initiates the punch, but resist the urge. Power can be created from any position as long as the internal body mechanics remain the same and the arms are connected to your centre. Once fluidity has been achieved it can easily be applied to a partner. Just make sure you are trying to use those simple contraction and expansions of the hips and shoulders to moves your mass at speed – after all this is the only way to create power!

I have uploaded video footage to my YouTube account to help explain the exercises. Please check out: http://youtu.be/PEMCtkQWAp4

So what are we trying to do in karate? Kumite is great for teaching us how to move, read an opponent and manage a fight. But *kihon* and kata, done correctly, teach us how to create power. Without this understanding, karate is simply about making shapes.

Steve Ubl Sensei once said that 'there is no such thing as basic techniques, only basic principles'. A very succinct and very accurate statement. In many dojo around the world I see people trying to make shapes that others will judge. Of course, this is not only inevitable, but vital as one progresses through the grades. However, you must reach a point when this is no longer the goal. We must all make sure that technique is only an external manifestation of internal movements. Shapes are a result of karate, not karate itself.

In conclusion, I remember the first time I accompanied Kagawa Sensei to England. John Cheetham, editor of *Shotokan Karate Magazine*, had invited Kagawa Sensei to teach in the UK. I was on the instructors' course in Japan at the time and so tagged along to translate. Over dinner John spoke about a debate that had arisen in articles and letters of the magazine regarding whether one's heel should be up or down when punching *gyaku zuki*, and how this affects power. John asked Kagawa Sensei what his thought were on the matter. Kagawa Sensei shrugged, he had no real opinion. I think he eventually said that is depends on the situation – 'case by case', as the Japanese are fond of saying. Sensei and I spoke afterwards and I commented on how I had never even thought about the whole 'debate' regarding heel up or down when punching. Kagawa Sensei said 'me neither'. The point is that any external movement is a result of internal actions. When punching, one must move one's centre (one's mass) at speed to the direction of the target. This target may be close, it may be far. The act of moving forward a small or greater distance will affect the external manifestations of the technique and although the shapes that are produced may be different, the fundamental principles remain the same – this is exactly what Kagawa Sensei meant when he said 'case by case'!

EIGHTEEN

New-Fangled Kata

In 2014 I had to reinvent my karate self. Over a decade of building a career abruptly ended; 80 per cent of my work was wiped out. I reverted to form, training, writing and teaching. This article was published in Shotokan Karate Magazine in mid-2014. Facing an existential crisis, it allowed me to reassess my focus and my resultant conclusions percolated out through several articles.

In the Shotokan syllabus we have the twenty-six pillars of our art: the twenty-six kata that were set down by Nakayama Sensei when the JKA was established. From these forms, we have drawn all our techniques, which represent classic Shotokan karate, and through these kata we can trace our history back to the beginnings of martial arts. Surely no one would argue these points? We have all we need, right? There is no necessity to study any other kata! In fact, some people advocate that we should take five years to study just one kata. We don't have the time to study any more, correct?

Why does Kanazawa Sensei teach *Gankaku-sho* and several *Goju Ryu* kata? Why did Nakayama Sensei teach non-JKA/Shotokan kata at his private Hoitsugan Dojo? Why does Asai Sensei practise over 120 different karate kata? Why do *Shito Ryu* karata-ka have over fifty kata in their syllabus? And where do we get a large amount of karate techniques that are not found in the twenty-six kata (*Ushiro-geri* being the most obvious)?

I was a member of the Japan Karate Shoto-renmei. As a member my karate, and the direction of karate within the JKS, was been heavily influenced by our chief instructor, Tetsuhiko Asai 9th dan. He was, and we are, pure Shotokan karate-ka. As I mentioned before, Asai Sensei knew and regularly practises over 120 kata that he has learnt and mastered in his fifty-two years of karate practice. The JKS no longer has twenty-six kata in its syllabus; Asai Sensei added five more, Junro one to five (more about this later). I am now a member of the WTKO – we practise beyond the twenty-six. Richard Amos, our chief instructor, trained for a decade with Asai Sensei and as a result many of the non-syllabus kata are taught, practised and cherished. But why did Asai Sensei do this and why do/did other top instructors feel the need to go beyond our 'twenty-six pillars'?

With the increased practice of non-Shotokan kata, I have heard concerns about karate-ka becoming Jack of all trades but master of none. Well, I would dispute this. In my twenty years of training around fifty-five kata, some I still practise and teach to this day, others I have learnt, taken from them what I feel is important, and then forgotten them. I am convinced that these non-Shotokan forms complement syllabus kata and karate as a whole. Each one has unique lessons to teach. Body mechanics that may only be hinted at in Shotokan kata, may take centre stage in the non-Shotokan kata. Once learnt and practised, I find that when returning to the syllabus kata I have a new depth of understanding and greater skill at performing them.

I understand that some people may not have the time or the interest to study more than the twenty-six required kata. However, for anyone who is going beyond the low dan ranks, then a greater, in-depth study of these kata would be beneficial. It also keeps the mind fresh. After *sandan*, what is new about karate? We all have the perfection of technique to aim for, but many people struggle to form short- and medium-term goals. These kata can be part of the answer. Plus, when the JKA formed, the exclusion of many kata seems arbitrary and unfair. I am no karate historian, so I will not pass comment on why some kata were chosen and others not, but after studying beyond the twenty-six I find it strange that *Gankaku Dai* was kept (known as *Gankaku*), but *Gankaku Sho* was left out. *Meikyo Shodan* was kept (known a *Meikyo* or *Rohai*) but *Meikyo Nidan* and *Sandan* were discarded.

So I would like to bring to the attention of the readers a few kata that they may find interesting (all of which can be viewed on YouTube.)

Rantai: It means 'difficult body' and is mostly a kicking kata. Introducing *ushiro-geri* and *ura-mea-geri*, the kata is great for developing strong and flexible hips.

Hachimon: It means 'eight gates' and takes its name from the eight directions it takes throughout the kata. Helping to develop strong, fluid turns and pivots, this kata is great for concentrating on the fundamentals of stance.

Meikyo Nidan: The second out of three. Whilst complimenting *Meikyo Shodan*, it is similar to the *Tekki* kata. When I first leant *Tekki Shodan*, I found it difficult and complicated. Later, when I learnt *Nidan* and *Sandan*, I understood how basic *shodan* was, but at the same time learning *Nidan* and *Sandan* gave me more insight into Shodan. *Meikyo* is the same. After practising *Nidan*, *Shodan* seems simple and undemanding, whilst at the same time you gain a greater appreciation of it.

Kakusen Shodan: One of seven. This is an *ashi-bari* kata. It teaches so much about balance, strength and timing; it is a great way to practise foot sweeps.

Senka: It means 'line of flowers'. There are no straight lines in a row of flowers, nor are there in *Senka*. A wonderful kata, concentrating on correct pivoting, turning and spinning with the deployment of *kime* at the end of each turn.

Joko Issei: One of five. A basic kata to help with pivoting and the use of hips to generate body movement.

Junro Shodan, Nidan, Sandan, Yondan & *Godan*: Five kata developed by Asai Sensei. *Junro* means to 'level up' or 'the next step' and each one is designed to bridge the gap between low/intermediate kata and the advanced kata in the Shotokan syllabus. These kata complement the existing twenty-six and as a professional instructor, they have given me a mass of ideas that I can translate into *kihon* and kumite lessons.

Funakoshi Sensei taught fifteen kata. Nakayama Sensei added eleven more and taught even more at the Hoitsugan. Kanazawa Sensei teaches *Gankaku-sho* and *Goju Ryu* kata. Asai Sensei draws from his vast wealth of knowledge and will teach non-Shotokan kata depending on what weaknesses he sees in his students. They must all think that there are advantages to going beyond the twenty-six standard kata and I can see why. Each kata has unique insights into biomechanics. Even if we practise them for a short time and then forget them, our bodies have muscle memory, which will then be used when we practise standard forms. Furthermore, these kata haven't been 'Shotokanised'. Over the years small changes haven't been made for the sake of competitions and gradings. They are in their original form and as such, the *bunkai* to each kata is both practical and efficient. There is no need to change the kata to make correct distance with your partner. Nor is it necessary for your partner to attack unrealistically short as you step in to block. They really work and I have often taught these kata initially through *bunkai*, then have my students add all the pieces together to make the kata; something I would never dream of doing with Shotokan kata.

Karate has progressed so much since it was first introduced to the West over forty years ago. I think the increasing practice of these non-Shotokan kata represent the strength and development of our great style.

NINETEEN

Onwards and Upwards

As a professional instructor I have always been desperate for new ideas. I often felt some of the conflict I experienced in the later years of being part of the JKS was due to me training with and inviting to teach for my group non-JKS instructors. But I was always searching for greater depth.

When I left the JKS and explained my new direction on Facebook, I finished the post with Onwards and Upwards. There were no winners with what happened at that time, but I was exposed to many new ideas within the WTKO. I am thankful for my time there and in many ways this article resulted from several conversations with Richard Amos Sensei.

I recently had the pleasure of teaching in North America. There was a double bill of me and another chap, an instructor of some renown within the group I was teaching for. Not without talent, this instructor had been many times national kata champion and moved with fluidity and grace.

I had an opportunity to watch some of his classes. He was a knowledgeable and engaging teacher, but I have to say his classes were all a bit samey. Focusing on kata, he seemed to break forms down and crowbar meaning into them, to what end I am unsure. Of course, some sequences were interesting and thought-provoking. There were a few moments when I thought 'Oh, that's nice' and 'Yes, I'll nick that one, thank you very much.' But a whole weekend of endless routines? Clever? Yes. Interesting? Maybe. Educational? Well, the jury was out. Were the array of *kyu* and dan grades educated by the sessions he taught? Had they improved or received information that would allow them to develop as karate-ka? Or did they leave having practised hundreds of patterns, none of which would ever be remembered?

It reminded me of a Billy Connolly gag, when he would predict to his audience that, after the show, someone was bound to ask what it had been like: '"Hilarious," you would reply. "Oh, yeah. What did he say?" your friend would ask eagerly. "Err ... no idea," you'd concede after considerable thought.'

Watching a stand-up comic doesn't make you funny, just like watching – even briefly practising – a whole series of applications doesn't make you good at karate. The attendees of the above-mentioned seminar left having enjoyed classes from this talented and humorous senior and I am sure he will be invited back to teach more. However, whilst travelling home it occurred to me that over recent years I have often seen this type of class.

For years we were subjected to the 'Harder, Faster, Stronger' instructors, bellowing out superlatives, pretending it was teaching. These types of sensei seem to be a dying breed as students abandon such dojos, either giving up completely or moving on in search of some proper *budo* information ... and I have to say, perhaps this is a shame. In such dojos, you never saw rotund, cumbersome black belts. They were always populated by keen, fit karate-ka. Maybe they lacked an understanding of certain core principles, but at least they trained hard and were strong.

Now we often see dojos that have instruction of a much more intricate nature. Like my fellow camp instructor from America, they break kata down, giving endless possibilities to certain moves in a sequence from their favourite kata. However, for me, this is equally uninformative because it isn't based on principles. I have had the pleasure to train with such instructors as Steve Ubl and Yutaka Koike who have taught kata through application. Their approach (and something I have tried to incorporate in to my own instruction) is that application is merely a device to support the core principles that the kata is trying to teach. I recently had a conversation with Richard Amos about the very same issue and he believes that *bunkai* must adhere to three principles: 1 Do not add or take away a technique; 2 The application must be realistic; 3 The solo performance of the kata should be enhanced by one's understanding of the bunkai.

I couldn't agree more. With these concepts in mind any application practice should always bring classes back to correct, principle-based training.

So why is it that talented karate-ka resort to convoluted and elaborate routines that resemble a whole new kata, with the added difficulty that is has to be done in unison with an equally unsure partner? Living in Ireland, this way of practising reminds me of Kempo Karate. Although I know Ed Parker's brand of budo exists throughout the world, through a strange quirk of history it is one of the most widely practised martial arts in Ireland. I have a student whose family on one side are all Kempo Masters. His uncle is a Grand Master 9th dan, and Semi Grand Masters and just plain Masters percolate out from this uncle like a family tree within a family tree. My student, now a very capable 2nd dan and black sheep of his Kempo-loving family, often comes to the dojo with stories of how one family member or another has reached 'Sublevel 4' – google it to see the complexity of their drills. On first glance it look interesting, something different from our normal *gohon* kumite. But it's like learning a language parrot fashion; that is to say, learning stock phrases like 'Where is the station?' The problem with learning a language like this is that no one ever conveniently replies, 'The station is over there.' Learning a great number of drills doesn't give you depth of knowledge, only breadth. There is no refinement of the principles, there is no development. If we take the analogue further, learning *gohon* kumite is similar to studying a language properly: learning grammar, vocabulary and syntax. Learning to move forward and back with fluidity whilst keeping your core engaged, learning how to judge distance, learning how to maintain controlled relaxation until the last moment of *kime*. These are all principles that can be applied in the most simplistic of kumite drills right through to real-life situations. And, more importantly, these principles can forever be refined, continually deepening one's understanding of Shotokan.

So why is it that talented karate-ka have rabbit-warrened down this cul-de-sac of knowledge? I am unsure. Are they in search of further obvious meanings to the art they practise? Have they not been given the tools to explore the minutiae of basic technique? Is it because our art, by definition, is esoteric, that is to say aspects will only be revealed when the practitioner is ready?

I have seen great competition fighters abandon traditional karate and move on to MMA, believing (wrongly) that karate isn't genuinely effective. My colleague from America, a great kata competitor in his day, has done a similar thing, moving into the kata-based MMA, albeit a type that isn't particularly challenged, unlike the competition fighters who ground and pound regularly. For me it seems a shame. There is more within traditional karate. So, what is the answer?

I have referenced principle-based training a few times in this article, that is to say whatever training we are doing, it must be to help further refine the principles that underpin Shotokan. There is no such thing as basic technique, only basic principles. What we consider basic techniques are merely the physical manifestations of basic principles. Whether we are doing *kihon*, kumite or kata, whether we are doing free sparring or *bunkai* drills, our training must be driven by the desire to understand and refine the principles at work. There is only a small number of physical principles, but they should be referenced at all times. As a result, things start to change.

First it becomes obvious that there is never one correct way to do something physical. Principle-based training will produce an infinite amount of physical results. No two karate-ka will look alike as everyone's body is different. Great instructors often fall into a trap of expecting their students to move like they do. They fail to see that they are great instructors, often in no small way, due to their natural physical ability. Whatever their forte, it is often a result of an innate ability that has been honed over years of dedicated training. Their movement represents the far end of the spectrum of what is possible. Most people fall into the middle of the spectrum and will never be able to emulate their instructors. But as long as good basic principles are adhered to, progress will be made. Once we realise that it is the principles we are trying to refine, we transcend the physical need to go faster, harder, stronger. Nor do we futilely try to copy our instructor or their physicality. Once we are on this path, we gain the ability to continually develop, refine and understand the art many of us have been doing for decade. So, onwards and upwards!

TWENTY

Connections

By 2015 I was writing very little about karate techniques although this piece, I feel, begins to distil the previous two decades of thoughts into a more concise article.

Many years ago I wrote an article for SKM about the importance of snapping one's shoulder when punching, blocking or striking. At the time Kagawa Sensei was emphasising this point in his instruction of basics and I felt it was an issue well worth highlighting. That was a decade ago, but recently I have been focusing on this aspect of my karate a little more. What I said in that original article, for me, still holds true. A decade later I feel I have more to say.

In 2007 I trained with Steve Ubl Sensei for the first time. An 8th dan, he is the Technical Director of the World Traditional Karate Organisation, a graduate of Nishiyama Sensei's Instructors' Course and was the first ever student of Nakayama Sensei's personal dojo, the Hoitsugan. He talked about connections within the body; that is connecting one's body weight to the technique. I vividly remember him mimicking countless students within the packed dojo, stepping forward and punching. 'Don't punch with the arm' as he stepped forward and then flicked out his limb with obvious flimsiness. 'Punch with the body' and some unsuspecting victim would be 'Ublised' with a one-inch punch that would make Bruce Lee proud.

In 2011 I was recommended by my *sempai*, Yutaka Koike, to invite Paolo Bolaffio to teach for my group in Ireland. He had been the right-hand guy for Shirai Sensei in Italy for many decades before leaving, travelling extensively in the East before returning and forming his own group, Makotokai. He delivered a breathtaking seminar, full of little gems of knowledge, given freely in his relaxed teaching style, and the underlying principle of his class and his karate was this connectedness. Reinforcing what Steve Sensei had initially said back in 2007 and the subsequent numerous times I had trained with him after that, the idea of body connection was fundamental to these great karate-ka – it made me think a lot about the development of my own karate.

Modern karate-ka have the odds stacked against us. Like many people reading this article, competition has played a part in my karate development. Whether it be your *raison d'être* or simply a rite of passage, competition is important. However, fundamental to what we must do, in the dojo and in a competition, is the use of *sundome*, the control and snap back of any strike. As a result, our techniques can go unchallenged. For some karate-ka, this may last their entire life, practising without actually hitting anything full force. One of the strengths of Shotokan is the amount of *kihon* we do – hours of honing correct form, which produces correct body mechanics, which produces power. But one of the weaknesses of Shotokan is the amount of *kihon* we practise – practising techniques, body mechanics that are never challenged. It leads to just making shapes, which is the problem I dealt with in my *SKM* article.

I have taught many black belts in my dojo and others whose wrists buckle when hitting a pad or whose *mae geri* fails to have any meaningful impact with the target, even when kicking at full force. The issue here is the level of connectedness of one's body weight to the weapon. We create power by combining speed and mass. Of course, speed is more exponentially important that mass, but speed alone just produces flicking techniques of little consequence. This is why both Steve Sensei and Paolo Sensei go to great lengths to emphasise connectedness. I feel this is fundamental to what karate is, the synchronisation of our body to create devastating power. Recently I have become fond of saying 'speed is ego, timing is karate'. What I mean by this is that people always want to punch fast and kick high – but fast techniques can hide a multitude of mistakes. Performing a technique slowly and correctly can often be far more challenging and this is not merely about muscle control and strength, it is predominantly about synchronising and aligning your body. Kumite is great at teaching us distance and timing, but *kihon* teaches us how to create power. A karate-ka can be awesome when moving, evading an opponent and placing herself in the perfect position, but if they don't have an impactful technique in their arsenal it's not really karate.

So, how do we do it? I think the two main areas in which people lack connectivity are the lats and the glutes. The wrist often buckles when punching but a little *makiwara* or bag work will remedy this.

Shu-Ha-Ri – Evolving Karate Thoughts

At first glance Photo 34 & Photo 35 may look almost

identical, but what I want to show and highlight is the connection of one's arm to the torso. At a very superficial level, this can easily be checked by the position of the punching arm's elbow. In Photo 34 my elbow is pointing outwards. In my experience the vast majority of people practising karate today will practise with a punching arm in this position. In itself it isn't that important, but it's often representative of a lack of connection with the lats, which allows the shoulder to over-rotate and disconnects the speed of the arm to the weight of the body. In Photo 35 I am showing an almost identical punch, this time with the lats locked in on the point of *kime*.

This is important as it means the technique is far more impactful ... and as a side effect, the elbow points down. It is my goal, when training, to maintain this connection at all times. But please don't take my word for it. Try hitting a punch bag or focus mitt that has weight behind it (i.e. not someone holding a mitt in their hand, which just flies away on impact, but held to their chest, so you can feel the power being transferred). Try hitting it with *tate ken* and with a normal punch. The vast majority of people will feel that *tate ken* is stronger, more impactful. This is not because *tate ken* is inherently stronger, but because when punching this way, the lats are still engaged, the elbow is still pointing down.

If we move our attention to the second key point of connection, I think I will remind many readers of countless lessons when instructors have told us to tuck our tailbone in and squeeze our abdomen. Using our hips without connecting the power source of our legs and hips to our upper body is like revving an engine without engaging the gears. Squeezing your tailbone with your core muscles, whilst locking in the glutes, produces a solid connection from the floor, through the legs and to the upper body.

Shu-Ha-Ri – Evolving Karate Thoughts

If we look at photo 36, what I have done is make a simple *Zenkutsu-dachi* whilst having my outstretched arms against the wall. From this point I simply lift my front leg up, maintaining the exact same back leg and torso angle. If you are driving forward with the abdomen and glutes, holding this position for more than ten seconds becomes difficult indeed – if it isn't, you have changed the angle and are simply leaning against the wall! This exercise is a very simple way to check the connectedness of your stance.

The next exercise takes this a step further by checking the connection of the lats as well. In Photo 37 I have simply made a *gyaku zuki* position close to the wall, engaged my abdomen, glutes and lats and then lifted my front leg. Trying to avoid twisting offline is exceptionally difficult, but truly challenges the muscle groups that are engaged when making connections.

My final point of this article is the idea of *shime*. Within Shotokan, this seems a very under-taught, and as a consequence, misunderstood, concept. But in other styles of karate it is an integral part of power creation. In Japan I would often be told to 'close my stance' (*tachikata o shime*), but explanations never went beyond that, followed by a kick up the arse. However, the concept of *shime*, I feel, needs greater analysis.

At its most basic, *shime* means to close. Closing one's stance can be easily explained as squeezing your inner thigh muscles. But it is more than that. I often think of *shime* as the internal form of *kime*. *Kime* can be seen and heard with the snap of a dogi as we fire out a kick or the pull back of *hikite*. However, there is a sense that all *kime* originates from internal *shime*. Without this anchoring of the stance or the engagement of the core muscles, then whatever is done with the limbs becomes a flick and lacking impact. Try this: make *gyaku zuki* and have a partner with an impact mitt on their chest stand on pace in front of you. Step forward to target without moving the upper body (in effect moving to *oi zuki*.) See how much power you can create. See what buckles and where that energy (body weight moving at speed) goes. The goal of the exercise is to transfer your body weight at speed through the knuckles of your fist. Although your arm isn't moving to add extra speed, power creation is still more than possible. At the point of impact make *shime* (close your stance). This then leads to locking in the lats and then wrist to produce a very connected (and therefore powerful) technique. You can almost feel that there is a tactile feedback from the punching hand, so that as your relaxed fist hits the target, this sends a message to make *shime* in the stance, then lats and finally the wrist and fist to produce the external version of *shime*, which is *kime*.

Karate is constantly evolving. I hope my students will be better than me! In recent decades the development of the WKF and sports karate has revolutionised the way people do and think about karate. It has had a tremendously positive impact on what we do. However, we must always try to guide our development and be mindful of lessons that have already been learnt. Ultimately, karate technique is about creating power but speed is vital – and that speed must be connected to our body weight to create truly centred movement. For me, this is what the application of karate technique is truly about.

TWENTY-ONE

Shu-Ha-Ri Part II

(MOVING ZEN VS KARATE STUPID)

This article was published very shortly after I left the JKS and speaks for itself. Four years later, it is still very raw.

In the spring of 2006 I wrote an article entitled 'Shu-Ha-Ri' whereby I set out to explain the ideas of the Japanese way of learning a system (Shu), internalising a system (Ha) and going beyond the system (Ri). It got good feedback – so I thought it was time for a follow-up.

Youth is wasted on the young, but wisdom is wasted on the old – eight years later I feel a little more experienced, maybe even a tad wiser. Over recent months I have had a rather public divorce from the organisation I called home for many years and subsequently published a book that attempted to reveal my very personal story with said group. This article is in no way a response to recent events, although it would be true to say it has been inspired by recent happenings.

Shu-Ha-Ri – Evolving Karate Thoughts

Last week I watched a documentary called *Unbelievers*, a film chronicling the tour by Richard Dawkins and Laurence Krauss. These two eminent scientists travelled the world giving lectures 'in conversation' with each other – a kind of free flow of ideas between the two of them whilst an audience watches: a spectator sport for academics.

During the documentary Dawkins remarks how in today's world there are no taboos. We can talk about politics, money, sex – nothing is off the table as far as our critical minds are concerned. However, for the religious amongst us, the remaining taboo is God. The Creator's authority is never questioned in the same critical way. His very existence and everything that is associated with that is accepted to a point where creationism is taught in some parts of the world as an equal and competing alternative to evolution.

What, you may say, does this have to do with Shu-Ha-Ri? Eight years ago I set out my stall – I believe that karate-ka should be on a progressive trajectory, 'Onwards and Upwards' as I have recently become fond of saying. This is a belief that I hold dear. However, it is a belief that I feel has been hard-earned. When I first moved to Japan I went to meet my heroes – my karate gods – to train at the feet of giants, to learn from the source. I successfully entered the instructors' course and started to train alongside them. As I have very openly written both in *SKM* and *Karate Stupid*, this was challenging and many sacrifices had to be made. However, training and completing the instructors' course taught me only a few simple things. I learnt about myself and found that we are all capable of resilience beyond our imagination. More importantly I found that my heroes were normal men!

'May you never meet your heroes' is often a blessing, a wish, a hope. I, however, was delighted I had a chance to meet mine. From the outside, one can bestow superhuman qualities on our heroes, provide them with qualities that you believe they must have to attain the level they have achieved. I learnt this was false. They were human, they were normal men. Some may find this disappointing, a let-down – for me it was liberating. I have never seen people train as hard as my sensei and *sempai* on the instructors' course. They were ordinary men training in extraordinary ways. For me, my heroes became worthy of even greater respect. To be the strongest in the world when you have superhuman powers is easy. To be tough when you are the biggest is no achievement. But to push yourself beyond what anyone else thinks is possible, to be brave when you are the weakest in the room, this is true greatness and these people had it in abundance.

When I returned home I was eager to share my revelation; mostly it wasn't well received. In one particular case I was teaching in Israel. I was a thirty-year-old *yondan* and during an evening out with senior grades one *rokudan* in his fifties commented on how the Japanese are culturally advantaged to Westerners because they sit on the floor. As a result, they have greater flexibility in their hips. I piped up: I commented on how much instructors stretch in Japan; in fact, I continued, Kagawa Sensei, who started karate at eighteen years old, was really inflexible and, whilst being 'encouraged' by his *sempai*, had to work very hard to achieve the splits.

'Nonsense.' With a wave of the hand, the *rokudan* dismissed what I had to say. I was a bit taken aback – surely knowledge is power?

Ishikawa Sensei (the main instructor on the camp) took me aside. These guys, he told me in Japanese, had trained with Nakayama Sensei. They had history and lineage. They also had a very dogmatic set of beliefs – it was maybe best if I didn't challenge them.

In a similar way, I experienced this response in many other countries and dojos I visited. The Japanese were superhuman – case closed; that is why they are so good. I spoke about different training methods, ideas of strength training, tube training, *tetsu geta* (iron shoes) training, etc. but most of it fell on deaf ears. I started to understand: people need heroes; they want to believe in magic. To say to people you can be as good as senior Japanese instructors is uncomfortable because the uncomfortable fact is that the reason they aren't as good is because they don't train as hard. Giving our heroes superhuman qualities gives us the excuse to not achieve their levels. It is comforting and reassuring and echoes the sentiment in the aforementioned documentary when Richard Dawkins commented on Karl Marx's view that 'religion is the opium of the masses'. Being solely responsible for yourself is a truly brave stance to take.

But we are karate men! Surely we are brave, fearless, pushing ourselves beyond what normal civvies are used to? Maybe not. When I left the JKS many moved with me, many did not. This is unimportant, what is important is the rationale behind this. The why's, where's and what for's are merely gossip for us karate nerds. What I find interesting is the 'last taboo' within the traditional karate world. Just as 'Unbelievers' pointed out about religion, the connection to Japan, for some, is the most important aspect of their karate. In one specific case I had a couple of students who trained with me exclusively in morning training. In what is basically my own personal training, senior members of my dojo train three mornings a week, pushing ourselves in a similar way that is done in Japan. But for two individuals, their connection to Japan was more important than the training. When I left the JKS they left the dojo, to train alone, just to maintain a connection to their heroes. I am sure there was a whirlwind on cognitive dissonance behind their decision and nothing is simplistic, so we all must find our own path and I respect that. However, at the core of their decision and of this article is the taboo that is: if you are not connected to Japan are you really doing karate?

Here I must tread carefully. I don't want this to deteriorate into a diatribe about recent events but it is important to acknowledge the variety of feelings I went through and the conclusion that I came to regarding my move to the WTKO. I do not wish to discuss the decisions that the JKS made regarding my case – there are many truths and mine is only one of them. But it is important to discuss how this connection to Japan purveys our traditional karate world. Japan suspended me for almost two years, forbidding me to work outside my own dojo. Their rationale was that we must be connected to Japan to exist in an authentic, legitimate karate world. This belief is held not only in Japan but elsewhere – a belief can only have longevity if it is supported by a critical mass, in this case affiliated dojos and karate-ka around the world. For them, it was inconceivable that I would have another option.

I didn't buy into this worldview. For many years I had been teaching both at JKS-affiliated dojos and also independent or non-Japanese based groups. A great example of this is the group I often teach in Norway. I first had the pleasure of teaching the group in 1995. At that time they were affiliated to the JKA (Asai Sensei fraction) and I travelled with the UK-based Kato Sadashige Sensei to assist on their summer camp. They had a very high standard and during a period of my life where I was following Kato Sensei across Europe, this course sticks out in my mind as a highlight. A decade later I was asked back to be a main instructor on the still-popular camp. By now their connection with Japan had been severed. The main instructors were Richard Amos, Aidan Trimble and Tom Kompier – I was drafted in as a fourth instructor because the camp had grown so big. Last month I just completely my tenth consecutive camp and I look forward to next year, which will be twenty years since I first visited Norway.

So, back to Shu-Ha-Ri: my point is that my worldview has been greatly affected by groups like this. They are WTKO, gradings are supervised by Richard Amos and the standard of the karate-ka are of the highest I have seen anywhere in the world. Many of their members compete for the Norwegian WKF National Team and they are, in any measurable way, world class. And fifteen years ago they questioned the perceived wisdom of being connected to Japan. Their conclusion was to grow up, to follow Shu-Ha-Ri.

My path, my Shu-Ha-Ri, has lead me away from Japan. I am now a member of the WTKO, 'The best of Japanese Karate, without Japan' is the tagline of the WTKO GB & Ireland. It may seem a throwaway comment, but it isn't. My decision was, in many ways, forced upon me, although early as two years ago I was talking about stepping back from the group I had created because I saw this as the next step of my trajectory. Situations change and we must always be pragmatic: change is inevitable, but progress is optional.

I don't want to argue for a disconnection from Japan. I still have many contacts there and plan a trip with my students next year. It is a wonderful place full of fascinating history and great karate sensei. What I do want to argue for is that we allow ourselves to continue our development and not let our preconceived ideas of what karate must be prevent us from doing the best karate we can. There are fantastic karate-ka in the world; some in Japan, some outside.

A conversation I once had with a senior instructor in Japan really highlights what I believe is the stumbling block of many practitioners around the world. This instructor had gone through the instructors' course in the eighties. He had trained for many years with Nakayama Sensei, but had never had a conversation with him – in fact Nakayama Sensei had never said one word to him. I spoke to this instructor about Steve Ubl Sensei, who was the first student ever to stay at the Hoitsugan, at Nakayama Sensei's personal request. Steve Sensei had visited Japan frequently for nearly two decades, spending extended time training at this infamous dojo, and had made copious notes of the many conversations he had had with Nakayama Sensei. Steve Sensei had once taught *Chinte* and had demonstrated an alternative ending from the three hops, something that he had learnt from Nakayama Sensei. I mentioned this to the senior Japanese instructor and referenced the source. With a wave of his hand, he had called it nonsense: how could this guy (Steve) have anything valuable to add to the karate lexicon?

Karate, for me, is about development, progress, learning: the instructor's response was disappointing. For balance, I should also mention another senior Japanese instructor, who was my *sempai* when I was on the instructors' course. He has taught extensively around the world and he was the one who introduced me to Steve Sensei. He sought Steve out and travelled to San Diego (Steve's home town), spending considerable time trying to absorb every ounce of knowledge that Steve freely gives. My *sempai*, too, believes the study of karate should be about progress or Shu-Ha-Ri.

So, to conclude this rather convoluted article – Japan is

great. What the JKA did for countless karate-ka around the world is immeasurable. What the JKS did for me changed my life and made my dreams come true. More importantly, what I learnt in Japan was Shu-Ha-Ri. You learn a system like a child. You internalise the system like a teenager. But one day you must become an adult.

TWENTY-TWO

The Thin Yellow Line

By the end of 2015 I had started to publish articles almost exclusively through my Facebook page. In this fast-food, instant-gratification world, writing an article that might be published six months later to an audience whose feedback you'll never hear had limited appeal compared to a Facebook post. The articles moving forward tended to be shorter, which was probably a good thing, and I enjoyed publishing work as it was still fresh on my mind.

The thin yellow line is fear! That fear that we all feel when we enter the dojo (or at least should feel!). Last year I made a return journey to Japan. After two long years away, I was keen to reawaken my Eastern side. We trained with various instructors at locations as diverse as modern, purpose-built dojos in local-authority sports centres to the ancient, original Keio University Dojo, which Funakoshi Sensei inaugurated.

Our last session in Tokyo was with the Tokyo Area

Veterans Kumite Group. Twice monthly these competitors, ranging from their forties to mid-seventies, meet and hone their competition skills. I'd had a week of going into new dojos, having to prove myself; something I hadn't had to do in Japan for a long time. As I walked to Wakoshi Sports Centre in northern Tokyo I convinced myself this last session would be fine. How hard could it be? Fighting a bunch of old guys, what's the worst that could happen?

I know Japan. I sense that when I walk into a dojo, people start to perk up with the smell of fresh blood. Walking into this dojo was like a bad western, all we needed was a good ol' boy to instantly stop playing the piano in the corner as everyone turned to stare.

We warmed up, did a few meaningless basics and then everyone 'mitted-up'. What followed was thirty minutes of *uchi-komi*, one-two kumite drills as the line endlessly rotated. After an hour of training, we were given a short break and the head instructor, Takakuwa Sensei, the current sixty-years-and-over All-Japan Kumite Champion, gave us a choice – kumite to the left, kata to the right. My tiring group of twelve had a choice. I sidled up to Simon Bligh, an old friend whose comic exterior belies a deep toughness. 'What do you think?'

'Kumite, of course.' Damn! I knew he would say that.

I gave people a choice. Half went one way, half trundled after me to the left. The guys on the right were treated to a delightful kata class from the current All-Japan Veterans Kata Champion. We on the left had a different type of education. What followed was an hour of non-stop kumite drills and freestyle. What's the worst that could happen? Some guy broke my nose at the start of the second session. I was allowed to attack any one-two combination, he kind of blocked and then countered with full force to my undefended, non-expectant nose as I passively took the counter. Break may be too strong a word for it. It was a gross dislocation. I continued on, only to be diagnosed on my return home.

Fortunately I was the only one to be on the receiving end of such shows of dominance and vengeance was sought as soon as the freestyle began. My merry band of fighters left with their heads held high. The kata karate-ka left without the same rush of adrenaline. In fact, some of my group were disappointed with the choice they had made. I said nothing, unsure how I felt.

Japan 2015 – WTKO members with Tokyo Veterans Group.

That was three months ago and it now occurs to me that we have no right nor authority to judge. I look on my friends and students who chose to practise kata that night and see no real difference between them and me (us). I was fearful. I instantly knew what the Tokyo Veterans were capable of. I have spent many long years in Japan and I know what the reaction can be when a group of *gaijin* walk through the door; after all that's why we go – to be challenged, to push oneself, to see if we have what it takes. I am also under no illusion that the very same feelings are pulsing through the veins of my

Japanese counterparts as a dozen big foreigners walk through the door. Unless you are a psychopath, we all walk along that thin yellow line of fear – anyone who says different is deluded or should be sectioned.

Whilst walking the line, one day you may steel yourself and test your mettle. Other days, facing the exact same challenge, you may balk at the idea and shy back into the group. That yellow line is very thin and who knows which side we will end up on. On that day, after a week of proving myself to a different instructor at a different dojo each day, I was ready for the easy option, ready to take, as a friend once put it, a 'mental health holiday'. However, I knew a man who wouldn't recoil, so I asked him.

My point is that all we need to do, as karate-ka, is to choose the challenging side of the yellow line more times that the easy side. That's the difference between people who are good, who can fight, and those who can't. No one is born being able to defend himself. By small, almost meaningless, decisions, step by step we become stronger and stronger. But no matter how strong you become, you are always walking that very thin yellow line.

TWENTY-THREE

Myths

This Facebook post was written towards the end of 2015. The WTKO GB & Ireland was developing well but after thirty years of being connected to Japan I was still searching for my place in this new karate group. In no small way, writing these articles became a way of processing all I was having to deal with.

Often we can think of a myth as a lie, some yarn that has been spun over generations. However, for the purposes of this mini article, let's use myth in a more proper sense, that is a construct, a conceptualisation of the world around (seen and unseen). When hunter-gatherers, swayed by the agricultural revolution, started to convene in greater numbers than their traditional 150-member villages, myths helped complete strangers have empathy and shared understanding for each other and the world. As a result of social empathy, cooperation was a happy by-product. Whether it be royal hierarchy, tax codes or, dare I say, religion, all of it is a construct of 'Homo Sapiens – the storytellers' in order for society to function. In the modern world we have the myths of the value of the dollar, the concept of a corporation being a person, or the fortunes of being famous – it is all a construct.

But what does this have to do with karate? Well, each community, group or association creates its own myths. The JKA became 'Keepers of Karate's Highest Tradition' shortly after the very public divorce from its then Chief Instructor (Asai Tetsuhiko) in the early nineties. Their myth is that they are the only true heir to Shotokan's legacy (opposed fervently by the Shotokai group). However, if you happen to stumble into a dojo in Okinawa, their myth is that mainland karate is watered down Budo, a derivative of the true Okinawan martial system. I am sure if you happen to mention Okinawan karate to a kung fu exponent, maybe she would scoff at the Japanese islanders' attempts at Budo; their myth is that the fighting monks of Shaolin are the true way. Perhaps there are yogis in the depths of India denouncing the misunderstanding of the Shaolin fighting styles – the yogi's myth is that they are the keepers of the highest tradition. My point is that no matter what community we are in, myths are created in order to produce group identity, consolidate links and induce social cohesion. These myths are inter-subjective – they can only exist if enough people buy into them.

Recently I saw on social media a video of a group of twelve karate-ka performing kata. It was part of a summer camp and the instructor started off by letting the students know that they were being filmed in order to broadcast the event, via social media, to 'let those not present see what they had missed'. They were in the middle of a park on a concreted sheltered area training in running shoes to protect their feet as it drizzled all around. Another recent post I saw was of another summer camp where one of the instructors wanted to thank the 200-plus members who attended the session whilst simultaneously posting photos of a dojo with fewer than seventy karate-ka. I don't want to pass comment on either event; that is not my concern. These two groups are creating their own myths in order to facilitate the group. But any good myth must reflect the reality it means to portray. It will only be supported inter-subjectively if enough people support it. As fewer and fewer buy into a particular construct perhaps the myths have to be inflated to keep the current believers engaged ... but with anything that is constantly inflated, eventually it will implode.

We must always be careful to make sure that the myths we create are a reflection of the reality we live. Once myths are created to skew reality for our own means, organisations often crumble. As Voltaire wrote: 'I know God doesn't exist, just don't tell my servant lest he stabs me in the night.'

TWENTY-FOUR

Post-Modernism

The year 2016 was a crazy one. This article was written before Brexit and before Trump's election. Obviously my small blog failed to have the desired effect on the collective electorate, but it does represent what I felt were the beginnings of a paradigm shift within certain areas of the karate world.

I recently taught in the UK on one of my frequent and enjoyable trips across the Irish sea. On this particular occasion the dojo head introduced me to one of her new students. Not clad in the normal white attire, it was unusual for an attendee of a technical seminar to not have been completely assimilated into our way of doing things. It was explained that this chap had many years of experience in many martial arts and was it okay for him to train? Of course it was. And off we set.

From the outset he decided to construe my instructions in his own, unique way. Informed by his years of mixed martial arts, he followed the class with a liberal amount of interpretation.

I let him be. He was training, being respectful and was a potential new student for the hosting dojo. But after several hours the class had shifted gear and instead of me directing the lesson, small groups of three had been made. The clusters of karate-ka around the dojo worked on and discussed points that I had given them. My MMA friend was with a couple of young 1st *kyu* and they seemed to be getting to grips with the principles under discussion. However, as time rolled on, there was a change in dynamics within their group and MMA chap looked to be going off on a tangent. After nearly three hours of training, we were discussing the need to 'dial in one's stance'. I had given the groups a few ideas and drills to help focus on this point and let them explore the ideas themselves. As I wandered round, answering questions, I noticed the hero of this story had decided to teach the two young 1st *kyu* how to sidestep and do a boxer-like upper cut. These two young kids needed to focus on the matter at hand in anticipation of their upcoming Shodan exam, so I wandered over and said to the group, 'Guys, can you please focus on the principle we are talking about?' The two youngsters responded with an '*osu*' and I walked off.

Within minutes, MMA chap had sidled up to me. 'I don't like the way you handled that!' He was irate. I gave him a puzzled look. 'This is the arrogance I've come to expect from senior traditional martial artists, so I just want to say thank you for the class, but I'm leaving ...' Of course there was more said, albeit quietly and discreetly. I explained that I expected attendees of seminars to follow along with the class, especially karate-ka who have important examinations in the not-too-distant future. He dismissed my response as arrogance and left the dojo, I guess, never to be seen again.

So why have I called this article 'Post-Modernism'? At the

end of the last century this term came to describe the school of thought that proposed that everyone's opinion matters. That there was no absolute truth, just merely our own truth, constructed by our own reality. Of course, there have been benefits to such a movement. It fights against elitism and strict hierarchical systems. But there is a downside. When I was a kid the authority of teachers and the professional elite was without question. If you wanted to get your passport photo verified you had to get a doctor, lawyer or police officer to sign it. Now if your kid fails an exam it's the teacher's fault, and anyone can validate your identity for Her Majesty's government.

I think it has led to a new reality where subjective, rather than objective, knowledge is paramount. In the recent European Referendum in the UK, Michael Gove MP actually said, when asked about the stance he had taken, 'We are sick of listening to these experts.' Donald Trump famously said to an attentive audience, 'I love the uneducated' and was rewarded with a round of raucous applause. Within the karate world we have seen the implosion of once dominant, Japanese-based groups, their previous unquestionable authority eroded away for some legitimate and some-not-so legitimate reasons. And then, in microcosm, we have our MMA chap who decided to tar me with the arrogant brush that he presumes all 'senior' traditional karate instructors hold.

I believe there are dire consequences to the abandonment of senior opinions and peer-reviewed thought. Is astrology better than astronomy? Are witch doctors more capable than trained surgeons? No! And why? Because this knowledge is not subjective, but objective; results can be reliably replicated. Karate is not dissimilar, based on solid biomechanics, and there are simply good ways and bad ways of doing something.

But how would it work if students decided when they were good enough to become black belts? How would it be if martial artists decided to cherry-pick from different styles, mashing them together and becoming a master of their new, hybrid way? Well, we know how it is because it is happening all around us. I have seen senior instructors decide upon their own criteria for their own rank exam and then perform this in front of practitioners of different styles. In a back-slapping dance a kung fu *expert* promotes a karate *expert* and then the whole dance is done in reverse. Similarly, the rise of MMA has produced 'masters' in the Jack-of-all-trades style.

Traditionalists like me can watch from the sidelines and scoff at the illegitimacy of such practice, but if we do I think we are in danger of succumbing to such developments. This post-modernism is a reaction to something. Within karate, for decades our art was controlled by an elite few. They were gatekeepers of knowledge and we had to acquiesce to their demands in order to have access to the information. This often led to the rise of demi-gods and the horror stories that we can hear in any dojo throughout the world. Of course there were many great, accomplished, good-natured pioneers of Shotokan. However, bad-tempered, money-grabbing, insecure and dominating sensei also populated the karate scene of the last century and still hang onto power by their fingertips well into this century.

As a result, many karate-ka decided to throw off the shackles of such constraints and form independent groups, promoted themselves to high levels and no longer felt they had to work within a community. In 2014 I left the JKS. At the time many friends expected me and recommended that I go independent. I never considered it an option. We always need *sempai* and sensei in our lives, someone to justify opinions to and draw inspiration from. We need to live in a peer-reviewed world where our tangent thoughts are not allowed to develop unchallenged. If we don't, there is a downside. Remember when a university degree meant something? Remember when achieving a black belt wasn't simply the unquestionable conclusion of several years' training? If we allow ourselves to slip blindly down this greased slope of post-modernism, we all suffer, we are all devalued.

TWENTY-FIVE

Multiverse

Towards the end of 2016 I think I had found a new confidence in what I wanted to talk about and how I wanted to say it. The WTKO GB and Ireland had grown significantly, and we had become a truly national organisation – although in order to continue living peacefully in Dublin, I have to acknowledge that the UK and Ireland are two very distinct countries. This article was born from the utter bewilderment as to why people just couldn't get on. For the vast majority of karate-ka, it was merely a hobby; nothing important enough to allow tribal warfare to erupt at an alarming frequency.

We live in the age of the multiverse paradigm. Boffins, who know better, tell us that there are multiple universes out there, each representing a different outcome of what could have been. So, let's imagine we have two worlds, Universe Baka and Universe Erai (get your Google translator out!). In both worlds there are two JKA, both developing karate in their own unique way.

Let's look at Universe Baka first. For various reasons they face a situation where the UK-based Kawasoe Sensei has been brought back into the group after many years on a different path. The decision to bring him back, made several years previously, has set a collision course for the two rival groups in countries where both the Kawazoe group and the JKA exist. Kawazoe Sensei affiliates were ordered, rather impotently by the JKA, to be subjugated by existing national bodies and when that never worked out, two rival JKA-affiliated groups emerged. It was the elephant in the room that karate nerds loved to gossip about. As this new route to the JKA gained momentum, the existing groups demanded something be done – after all they had rights to the brand, built up after years of loyalty and obedience … The eventual culmination of the collision course could be devastating, with there being no winners.

However, parallel to this world was Universe Erai. In this world, cooperation was the order of the day. This world realised that anything of real value, held up as noteworthy or cherished by society, was achieved through cooperation. When Kawazoe Sensei re-joined the JKA, it wasn't met by ego-driven reactions. People realised that Kawazoe Sensei was a huge talent and brought a wealth of knowledge back to the group. The affiliated heads around the world didn't feverishly protect their use of the brand name, they knew that their karate was more than just a logo. They felt confident in their position and within the JKA community. Now there was another JKA community in their neighbourhood – they weren't a warring rival, just another likeminded group that did the same sort of stuff. Confidence allowed them to make decisions that were best for the community, not ego-driven decisions made to protect the positions of a few community leaders. Every move was done with sustainability in mind.

So in Universe Erai the JKA grew. Of course, the old model of countries with one group, one chief instructor, one national team, one truth, had disappeared – gone as a new paradigm or way of conceptualising the world developed. As the internet democratised everything, the JKA was quick to adapt and accept this as an inevitable development. But of course they became stronger for it. Groups respected the journey that the other group had made. They neither sought to dominate them or convince them that their way was better – they saw them as cousins from another, similar community where cooperation on whatever level could only be beneficial to both sides.

So what does karate teach us? What is the dojo *kun* really saying to karate-ka? It would be great if we could live in the utopia of Universe Erai, but I fear most live in Universe Baka; and fear is at the heart of it. In the world of Budo, martial artists bicker about whose style is best – how Zen is that? In the karate world you are pigeonholed by your style. In the Shotokan world, split after split has defined the twenty-first century. Even in single international organisations there is infighting and backstabbing. Why? Fear? Insecurity? The need to be dominant?

But of course we are all human, driven by the wants and needs that ebb and flow through our bodies with the rise and fall of testosterone and other mind-altering drugs. It's such a shame, but true greatness, something that everyone can be proud of, only comes through cooperation. Maybe it's time the karate world has its own paradigm shift.

TWENTY-SIX

The Bubble

This was the last article I wrote whilst in the WTKO. Reading it again now, eighteen months after I first published it, I can feel my desire to hold on to the community, the direction, the ethos that we had all worked so hard to create. I was, in many ways, so different in outlook to many within the group, but that was okay. I thrived on the challenges of my positions because it led to progress and development. I actively looked for it, inside and outside of the community. I really wanted to explain why.

From the Breitbart-watching, alt-right loving Trumpeters on one side to the BBC-devoted, left-leaning Remoaners on the other, recent events have proven that we are all living within our own little bubble. Concourse between political parties, exchanging ideas and challenging pre-conceived ideas seem to be a thing of the past. Now the only disagreement that seems to take place is within one's own group about how one's hatred of one's rivals is bigger, better, stronger than others within one's clan. The world seems to have gone mad, deteriorating into playground squabbles were people simply sulk and walk off with their metaphorical football. Thankfully, not in the karate world, hey?

Last week I was doing my usual research for work. My wife calls it 'looking at Facebook' but I know the truth; I was searching for ideas, concepts and inspiration that I can bring to my own training and seminars. I stumbled across a video of Naka Tatsuya Sensei from the JKA. It highlighted a seminar he taught in Australia and it was great. The first day had been distilled to the essentials by editing and I sat through the thirty-minute presentation enjoying his delivery and its content. I was going to repost, but then never got around to it. I later pondered my apathy to click 'share'. Had it have been the highlights of a WTKO *sempai,* I am sure I would have reposted immediately, but not so with this video. I do so now (https://www.youtube.com/watch?v=y0LMSknvKVU). Watch it, it's great.

I've met Naka Sensei. When I first went to Japan in 1992 I trained at East Fire Dojo Summer *Gasshuku*. He had just won the All-Japan Championships and was on the camp teaching a little, but mostly training. We paired up several times and in my youthful naivety I thought, 'Jeeez, he's not bad!'

So, was it my bubble that stopped my immediate repost? Am I only interested in dialogue with others with similar logos embroidered on their dogi chest? Of course, not. For years, when part of the JKS, I took great pride in working with the likes of Richard Amos, Steve Ubl, Aidan Trimble, Kitagawa Takeshi and many others who didn't share the same affiliation (in hindsight, one of the many reasons I clashed with seniors at the hombu). Now that I am WTKO, I am happy to say that

that tradition continues and is encouraged. This is possibly why it came as a shock that I would allow my bubble to affect me in such a subtle way.

It got me thinking. The same can happen even within isolated groups where the hierarchy and structure is set, each tier within the framework providing a glass ceiling for those below. I am very lucky, I have a few people in my life who I call *sempai* and sensei who truly understand the depth of meaning behind those titles. I once saw footage of a police officer being harassed by a rather aggressive lady who was under the influence of something quite strong. The officer was trying to calm her, but the lady took offense and said, 'I'm going to report you to your superiors.' 'Madam,' he replied calmly, 'I don't have superiors, only seniors.' It stuck in my mind as being very articulate, clever and insightful in a moment that was exploding with stress. And isn't that statement so true? As my good friend Scott Middleton always says, 'Karate … the endless journey.' We are all on a journey, moving forward on paths that have a similar (but not necessarily identical) trajectory.

The aforementioned *sempai* and sensei challenge and test my ideas both in and out of the dojo, but it is done with the knowledge that we are all on our journey. In return, as a *Kohai*, I support and challenge, not from below, but from behind as I move forward. Wouldn't it be awful if we all lived within our own bubble; where opinions, positions and relations were set, fixed, unable to develop?

So, to conclude, whether you are a Trumpeter, Remoaner, *kohai* or *sempai*, what is important is that we are forever challenging our ideas and beliefs. By doing so, we inch forward on our path and hopefully enjoy the company of others on the way!

TWENTY-SEVEN

Micro vs Macro

Being expelled from the WTKO was heart-breaking. The whys and wherefores can be left for another time. As ever, I reverted to training, teaching and writing. My cathartic release started with this.

I'm sitting in the breakfast room of Roberto Nearon, here in Detroit, a lovely friend and senior member of the HDKI USA. I have known him many years and my annual visit to his home, family and dojo are always far too brief.

Last night, after a long transatlantic flight, we were sitting in Miller's Bar, our regular Thursday evening haunt in Michigan, with the waves of jet-lag starting to hit. However, the locally famous cheeseburger washed down with a couple of glasses of Blue Moon help see me through until bedtime. I am now awake and well rested after a good night's sleep and ready for a four-day, four-city tour of the USA.

The conversation last night meandered as any bar conversation should and halfway through the night I found myself quoting certain professors whose classes I had taken whilst reading social anthropology at university. There is a need in any community, culture or society to have very local connections. These micro-connections provide the framework of one's local network. Family is an obvious example of this: your mother, father, son or daughter. These are the people you rely on and who rely on you daily. This is the fabric of our inner life. Beyond that, we are connected to our wider family and community, our aunties, uncles, nieces and nephews. It is no coincidence that in colonial times the ruling British children would call the adults within their community auntie and uncle not because they were blood relatives, but in absence of family, this convention was adopted to make the community functional. And then, finally, beyond the family, we have our community: the local schoolteacher, the village butcher, the line of neighbours up and down the street, all sharing a shared myth of commonality that create the comfort blanket of society. But what, you may ask, does this have to do with karate?

Often I think that my dojo is my karate family. Brothers and sisters in arms, training hard, fighting the good fight. They are my confidants, my inner circle, the place where I can vent my frustrations and insecurities and explain my hopes and desires. Beyond that, I have my extended family – in my case the HDKI GB & Ireland. These are the guys I see most regularly. They are the aunties and uncles, the nieces and nephews in my pseudo-karate family.

Beyond that, we belong to a greater community, the HDKI, which has been recently created and will hopefully expand in a sustainable way. The community makes me happy and I know why. A common anthropological model for a successful – and by that I mean happy – community is when an individual has strong links in their home. This is then reinforced by a greater number of links within their local community, albeit it less frequent or pervasive. The final icing of the cake, so to speak, is for community members to have strong links to other communities. It allows for cross-pollination of ideas, creates niche groups and allows people to have a greater sense of belonging within the wider context of the world. If all these three levels of connection are achieved, society, in general, flourishes. Back in my JKS days I used to teach for a talented karate-ka in Loughborough, whose family were of Indian heritage. His family was quintessentially modern-day British Indian, blending the traditions, culture and heritage of the subcontinent with British society. I would often fly over Friday, teach Saturday and then fly back Sunday. The first evening we would spend down the local pub, playing pool with his work colleagues, talking football (which I had no idea about) and drinking beer. The next evening we would be eating 'sizzlers', wonderful Indian cuisine that I had never seen on the menu of any other Indian restaurant I'd been to. My anthropological training woke from a slumber of post-university amnesia and I could recognise the satisfying functionality of this snapshot of modern British culture. My friend had close, ethnically specific connections at home and within the close-knit community. He then had wider connections within the general community, within work and within the dojo. He then finally had a greater connection within the wider (karate) world being part of an international group. Life was working as it should.

But what happens when we miss an element or two? Imagine being part of a family who all live halfway across the world – the psychological effects of this on emigrants are well studied. Imagine being part of a close-knit family, but never leaving the four walls of the home, never exploring the variety of ideas, opinions and lives beyond the nuclear family. I think a functioning existence is a difficult balance to create and one small tilt in the wrong direction can easily topple you into dysfunctionality.

For karate-ka, independence can be an alluring option, free from the control of a dominating group, eager to regulate the minutia of the dojo's existence, but it also results in seclusion. Equally isolating is the choice to remain connected to the wider world when the local or national community have chosen otherwise. Both examples I have seen recently in my professional life and I empathise with the individuals involved, forced to make choices that only produces degrees of losing – there are no winners when a balance can't be reached. Of course, for a short time it is possible to give the illusion of a well-balanced community. Social media has a way of making the global village a reality. The ease of connection, with push notifications, a plethora of emojis and Google algorithms allow us to live within a bubble that is hard to burst. But the existential truth that we must face is that there is a need for authentic connection. A phone call from a friend or an *'osu'* from a training buddy are infinitely more valuable than a like from an acquaintance 3000 miles away. I truly believe that nothing can be achieved alone that cannot be bettered in collaboration. And as the African proverb says, If you want to go fast, go alone. If you want to go far, go together.

TWENTY-EIGHT

Structural vs Social Power

The creation of the HDKI was a challenge that I relished and embraced. I read, researched and investigated ideas that would help move the group in a sustainable direction. Checks and balances were vital and in no small way, I hoped, committing my initial ideas to paper at the start would be vital to make sure I kept true to that vision.

Recently, my professional life has been a bit tumultuous. That's not a bad thing, change is inevitable and over recent years I have become (mostly) quite adapt at embracing the schism, riding the emotional wave Zen-like rather than cowering from the tsunami. Lately, as the waters have started to calm, I've turned my attention to thinking long term about the organisation we have just created. I want to be part of a sustainable group that will run well after my planned early retirement! Therefore, I have been reading a little about organisational structure, authority and power. Not to get too geeky, but in 1959, French and Raven, two prominent social psychologists, proposed five forms of power:

No. 1: Legitimate power – describing people who have been elected to power.

No .2: Referent power – identifying the influence people wield in organisations and communities.

No. 3: Expert power – given to those in the know.

No. 4: Reward power – reserved for those who can give (and take away) privileges, credentials and legitimacy.

No. 5: Coercion power – the use or threat of force or expulsion to achieve desired results.
https://en.wikipedia.org/wiki/Power_(social_and_political)

Of course no one ever relies on just one form of power; the ebb and flow of group dynamics will always mean that relationships within our chosen community remain somewhat fluid. With the above-mentioned framework I started to think about groups that have been dominating the karate scene for some time. French and Raven determined that power is either endorsed by the structure that contains it (legitimate, reward and coercive) or is contained within the social relationships of the people involved (referent or expertise). We can see the structurally endorsed power as the rules, regulations and edicts that are dictated from above; socially endorsed power is based on relationships of trust, knowledge-sharing and mutual support. Karate is heavily dominated by the hierarchical system that percolates throughout our chosen field of leisure time. The kingpin, the chief instructor, the guy that was through the door first sets the tone of the group, dictates the rules of the association and polices the community. There may be a trickle-down of power with subordinates being allowed to create small chiefdoms where they too can implement their version of absolute power, but ultimately authority is wielded unchecked, respect is demanded and rules are dictated. In these groups seniors are superior – and, by consequence, juniors are inferior. We should ask ourselves, do these people govern because they have definitive expert power, or are they in the position because they have created a structure that preserves their position at the top and have the legitimacy to reward and coerce? Taking this idea away from the karate context and looking at it in the extreme (chart the course of any dictator) and you can see this shift of power played out in a very real and often catastrophic way, from euphoric populism to dark coercion.

As with global politics, I don't see longevity in this model. Modern technology gives us access to people, thoughts and content across geographical, structural and cultural barriers; organisations that operated within strict regimes are likely to have troubled futures.

I'd prefer to be involved in a group where social power is wielded; an association like this would be a different beast altogether. If we return to French and Raven's model, referent and expertise power would heavily dominate group dynamics in such a community. People would vote with their feet, endorsing the various leaders who would use the power they have received to influence and guide the group in a direction that is mutually beneficial and collectively endorsed. This may seem a little hippy, but in recent years there has been a paradigm shift in how corporations, businesses and organisations think about how their power structures work. (My identical twin brother runs a consultancy that deals exclusively with such matters and the academic letters after his name prove that it's a real thing! He was very influential when I created the structure for the HDKI.)

For me, this highlights the dominance of Expert Power. Is this important? Hell yes! Demonstrably, the old guard of well-established organisations initially derived their power because they were the best at the time, the highest grade, the first in the door. However, expertise has to evolve. So, what then, for the original leaders? Secure their position via a route towards structural power? Or take a leap of faith and rely on socially endorsed referent power?

I am a liberal-leaning, socialist hippy. When I put together the HDKI guidelines I told my good friend Simon Bligh that I felt like I had written the communist manifesto for karate. But I believe that structural power is transitory, elusive and will force those who wield it to forever incrementally tighten their grip on their depleting control. It is easily created and easily lost. Living in the bubble of coercing and rewarding members for following dictated decisions will hide the absolute truth that every decision made slowly eroded the foundation of one's power. I want to avoid this.

Although socially endorsed power is equally elusive and can also be lost in the blink of an eye, relying on one's expertise and referent influence within the community brings into focus the stark reality of organisational structure – one's authority is a gift from those who are directly affected by it. Misuse it and it can be retracted as quickly as it was given, but use it well and every decision made adds to the foundations that underpin the structure. The key to everything is trust. Within the karate context, the membership must trust the leaders to make the right decisions. Start to lose that trust and leaders will find themselves in a position of increasing illegitimacy. Power is not magically imbued within a title, it is hard-earnt, harder maintained and easily destroyed. We must constantly ask ourselves how the power we wield is operationalised and for these reasons, I think relying on socially endorsed power is the only model with longevity.

John Steinbeck wrote, 'Power does not corrupt. Fear corrupts ... perhaps the fear of a loss of power.' I have always looked for checks and balances in my life. As I move into a new chapter of my professional life I am very conscious of installing safeguards to prevent the insipid nature of even a modicum of power get the better of me. Like the physical aspect of my work, I am always looking for a new idea, an innovative approach, a third way. My hope and desire is that moving forward I can be part of a community that is truly sustainable – the dream of any left-leaning, social hippy.

I was expelled from the WTKO on a Wednesday evening. People gathered at my home and we discussed the implications until late. The Thursday was a whirlwind of emails, phone calls and me resting my head in my hands whilst muttering, For fuck's sake ...

That evening I asked another instructor to teach my regular class, I couldn't face the dojo. The Friday was St Patrick's Day and my family had already planned a weekend away – it was much needed.

And so the next time I found myself in the dojo was the following Monday, kata night. I set off teaching the ninety-minute class with a bit of *Bassai Dai*. Halfway through, one of the seniors asked a questions: should it be this way or that? I began my answer, but in the split second between being asked and answering, the situation hit me. This was the first time in thirty-two years of training that I had no senior above me, no external point of reference. I faced a row of black belts all expectantly looking in my direction. What I said may now be considered the correct way by those who had and would follow me. I never expected to be in this position and it was daunting.

I made a stupid joke – I find that to be the perfect temporary solution. I then explained, as far as I knew, the various variations. Then said, 'You are free to decide what is best for you.' I never want to lose sight of that. I am sure that the next two articles will be seen as personal slights on a number of instructors. They are not. They are simply me finding my way.

TWENTY-NINE

Training Mechanism

I am currently sitting in a comfy café in Bristol. I am three days into my rather long holiday from the dojo, but whilst my body idles its way to atrophy, my mind is not so compliant ... here I am, writing an article that has been coalescing at the back of my mind for some time now.

I have done it many times in the dojo, created or (more often than not) stolen a set piece that helps address certain challenges within my students' technique. I never underestimate my members' ability to ignore repeated instruction on one technical issue or another and tangent off down a cul-de-sac of sweaty grind that will ultimately lead to failure. So I often find myself readdressing such matters with a physical antidote, a drill that will focus so heavily in the opposite direction that balance is once again achieved. Recently, I have been fixating on our over-focus of driving into *shomen*. The driving from the back leg as we thrust out *gyaku zuki* really helps develop this deeply connected stance when making the ubiquitous punch. However, what about the same power being created when driving into *hanmi*? My classes now often start by repeatedly thrusting the body forward from a ready *neko ashi dachi*, driving a *kizami zuki* out whilst connecting to a solid *Zenkutsu-dachi hanmi*. Over time, balance within their stance is reached.

These physical drills are good to create that holistic body type; functional fitness and physical intelligence is achieved. After all, *kihon* is like weight training for the body. We learn basic principles through basic techniques but sometimes these training mechanisms can be far more conceptual. For example, I have heard some very good instructors talk about how the front leg should pull the body forward as we transition in *Zenkutsu-dachi* – there is no biomechanical process that would allow this to happen. Others, I have heard, talk about the connection of hip and hand and how they should both start at the same time – the obvious difference in the size (and speed) of one's body and fist and also the difference in distance that both have to travel, creates an infinite amount of possibilities that the simple statement 'they should start together' cannot possibly accommodate.

I take these two examples not because I disagree with them, but because I see their value as a way of conceptualising what we practise. Imagining that the front leg is pulling one's body forward, helps to focus on the need to squeeze the inner thigh muscle when transitioning. Thinking about sending one's hand with the hip impedes the creation of stiffness in one's shoulders and also prevents the poorly timed execution of *waza* were people step and then complete the arm part of the technique, almost as an afterthought. For years I have had between eight and ten different high-level instructors visit my dojo every year. Each come with their own unique take of our great art and deliver lessons that my guys find insightful. So many times, I have seen instructors teach a concept that I have taught on countless occasions. 'That was fantastic, so insightful,' is the normal verdict of my students, as I smirk, knowing that I can never be a king in my own kingdom. The beauty of training with many different instructors is that students are bombarded with a variety of ways to basically do the same thing. My point is that these training mechanisms are a necessity that help everyone along their own personal karate journey.

But there is a downside. Sometimes I have experienced how these training mechanisms have developed into undisputable facts. Often instructors, wittingly or not, allow their ideas, concepts and metaphors to become absolute truth about how to do something. The first time I taught in South America I was informed by some very senior karate-ka that pulling from the front leg was the only way to step forward in *Zenkutsu-dachi*. I found a door and had one instructor make *Zenkutsu-dachi* with his back to the frame. I asked him to lift his back leg off the ground and try to move forward. With just his front leg on the ground, forcing all his weight back as he 'leaned' on the door frame, the metaphor of pulling from the front leg was instantly proven as being biomechanically flawed. I had a similar experience with the hand and fist metaphor as well. On these occasions, the information is sometimes accepted and taken on board; other times it is met with less enthusiasm, as if I were attacking the groups senior instructors, undermining their karate foundations. I am not, I am simply pointing out that often a certain percentage of students just want to be told how to do something in absolute terms. They will take a drill, a concept, a throw-away comment and solely focus on it until it becomes an undisputed truth, at the cost of any other dissenting information.

When I was part of the WTKO one of the criticisms that

I heard of the group was that all the senior grades were so different. Richard Amos' karate was so different from John Mullins', which was so different to Steve Ubl's, which was so different from mine. My answer was that that was the strength. As I develop my own group, the HDKI, my aim is to have many voices within the association. The one thing that all our members have in common is that we are all different. How can I possibly provide teaching metaphors that will speak to everyone? Any thriving, developing, growing organisation must have varying and (sometimes) superficially contradicting voices. Otherwise it is easily possible to descend to a place where only one voice is heard, where training mechanisms become absolute truth, where karate no longer evolves and develops.

At the same time, I don't want to be swept away in a wave of post-modernism, where everyone's opinion is of equal merit. Of course, experts have earned the right to strongly advocate knowledge that has been acquired over decades of research; but we can only ever speak for and of ourselves. I know how my body works, so insisting that everyone else moves like me is only an exercise in ego. Be creative, be original, but never allow one's inspiration to transform into absolutes and always be aware of the unintended consequences that our little insights may incur.

THIRTY

Karate – Absolutely

I liked the term axiom. I disliked the dictatorial way of teaching ... And I wanted to plug my DVD. So I wrote this article.

I recently released a DVD, *Karate Principles*. In the DVD, and in so many of the seminars that I teach, I talk about there being no such thing as basic techniques, only basic principles. The *waza* we produce are merely physical manifestations of those principles. However, it would be understandable if, for the majority of people, their takeaway is that there are certain absolutes that we must follow within our training. I can easily see how talking about the guiding principles can lead to a belief in unshakable facts; I want to talk truth to my students and after all if truth is not absolute it is not truth at all. However ...

As an example, let's take one of the twelve principles I highlight in the above-mentioned DVD; the concept of *Seichusen* or 'centre line'. In essence, when we do karate, we must keep our back straight. From day one in the dojo we are told to maintain form and posture whilst transitioning. I have spent whole classes on the concept and have invented or stolen many training mechanisms that focus on this principle. But does this fundamental principle of physical movement apply to a *judo-ka*? A boxer? Do we maintain our centre line as we leap from attack to defence in *Empi*? Of course not. When we start to look for this principle in other martial arts and our own, we understand that it is not absolute – so why do we put so much emphasis on it?

In mathematics and some philosophical debate, we often use axioms – propositions that are assumed without proof for the sake of studying the consequences that follow. Within a system of thought, the axiom provides a platform that all other discovery can be built upon. For me, the guiding principles of karate are axioms. That is to say, they act like a framework in which to discover and, more importantly, develop one's physical intelligence; like a sapling given a protective wire fence to aid growth. However, like any highly structured framework, the once-guiding lattice can often turn into a cage, constraining the very thing it was designed to facilitate.

For many, this highly structured, heavily dictated structure can act like a comfort blanket, mitigating insecurity by focusing on *the* textbook version of *waza*, the one *bunkai* to kata, the specific grading combination that will automatically elevate them to the next level. Fortunately, for some this over-manicured, conformist, *autobahn*-esque travel along the path isn't what floats their boat. For some, decades of pounding the dojo floor, repeating combinations ad nauseam becomes the futile fight against atrophy; forever trying to recapture that fleeting moment in their twenties or thirties when everything felt strong, powerful and good. For me, as I meander through my forties, having a technique feel strong means that I am getting pointless bio-feedback from the flailing arm or leg. Having it feel powerful has no connection to creating force. Believing that it is good is the common by-product of punching thin air.

My good friend Rick Hotton burst onto the karate scene in early 2014. Since then he has taught seminars all over the world and has developed a large and loyal community that enjoy his lessons both in and outside the dojo. I'm sure many traditional Shotokan instructors look at his seminars and just don't get his popularity. For me, I believe it is down to the fact that (apart from his technique, a unique blending of non-Shotokan principles, his humour and style of teaching) he doesn't present absolutes. In fact, often is the case he starts his seminars with a mini-declaration: 'I'm just here to give you ideas … if you like them, I'm honoured. If you don't like them, that's fine too.' He then sets about sharing his hard-earned knowledge, rather that dictating the actions of his audience. In my career, I have taken many elements of my professional style from a vast array of instructors. The above I have happily taken from Rick. I believe at a certain level this message is vital and I attribute a substantial part of his success to this fact. Freeing people from the cage of the highly structured system of absolutes allows them to discover what the lessons they have learnt means to them.

Would I teach this way to lower grades? Absolutely not! In my dojo, regular classes are taught in a regular way. I must always be able to revert to classic form, the strict regime once again challenging my body and purifying my technique. I also never want to attempt to shortcut my students' journey. Directing them to learn my conclusions is an exercise in ego that makes the doomed presumption that we all share the same body type. As a travelling instructor I want to facilitate people along their *Shu-Ha-Ri* journey. I want to share my knowledge that they are freely able to accept or ignore. The beauty of Shotokan is its diversity. I look at past greats: Asai, Enoeda, Nishiyama, Kase and, of course, Nakayama – after many years of learning others' truth, they eventually presented their own, hard-earnt, considered truth. So let us facilitate our own unique development by seeing the spectrum of possibilities that should give us all the freedom to break free of the heavily dictated karate absolutes.

THIRTY-ONE

10,000 Hours

Rick Hotton Sensei often talks about being a seeker – someone constantly on the search for a deeper, broader or more nuanced understanding of what we do. I can relate. I am constantly watching, reading and listening to 'stuff'. I never know where the next 'ah-ha' moment will come from, but when it does, I find it so personally rewarding.

I recently was forwarded a fascinating talk at LSE by David Epstein. In it, and in the subsequent TED talk I watched, Epstein debunks the 10,000-hour rule concept widespread within the sports science world. But before we move on with this mini article, let me just give you broad brushstrokes of the ninety-minute talk.

Epstein argued against the accepted popular narrative that presumes it is the amount of training done by the gods of the Olympiads, rather than their innate talent, that results in medals, world records and glory. In Gladwell's 2008 bestseller *Outliers*, the 10,000 hour rule was unleased upon the world. The concept championed in that book was that elite performers, regardless of their chosen field of expertise, need 10,000 hours of practice to achieve mastery. The concept has percolated throughout the sporting world to the point where elite academies of sport have created training regimes that will nurture talent from grass-roots level right the way up to elite performance whilst accumulating exactly 10,000 hours of training. The research that it was based on was conducted by Dr Anders Ericsson of Florida State University. He studied ten violinists who had already been pre-selected for the prestigious West Berlin Academy of Music and found they had a mean average of 10,000 hours of practice before winding up in the respected musical establishment, although some had practised for as few as 3000 hours whilst others had twiddled their fiddle for as many as 17,000 hours. Dr Ericsson eventually wrote a paper (entitled 'The Danger of Delegating Education to Journalists' – says it all, really) distancing himself from the now widespread paradigm of thinking.

So what does this have to do with karate? Two thoughts emerged from these talks. The first was the idea that genes play a huge role in development. As a karate instructor I have, over the years, taught a huge number of students. Why do some become good and others don't? I desperately want to avoid answering my rhetorical question with 'It's down to natural talent.' Fortunately, Epstein was very careful to point out that there are many ways individuals can optimally respond to training. Coaching styles, intensity of drills, ways of training can all have a dramatically different effect on different people. What I extrapolated from that was that people respond differently to different instructors. As I have said in the past, it never ceases to amaze me the amount of times I have had a visiting instructor to my dojo who has taught concepts that I often talk about myself, only for some of my students to walk off the dojo mesmerised by this new and revolutionary input they have just received. Some students, it seems, receive information far more receptively in one way, whilst other students improve from instruction in a completely different way. The need to have a wide variety of good level instruction is, I think, justified by Epstein's ideas.

The second idea I took from this new information was the need to constantly challenge our perceived wisdom – we never want absolutism to masquerade as a pseudo-academic understanding of subject. Education is the realisation of one's own ignorance, to paraphrase Socrates. For many years I have heard sensei instruct karate in dogmatic terms, but the more I investigate, the more I discover my own ignorance, the more I realise the seemingly infinite possibilities that can result in good technique.

So to conclude this mercifully short article, I recommend you listen to the talk – it's worth taking ninety minutes out of your day for. I would also like to say that in the next four months I have five visiting instructors. One is tall, lanky even, but with great core strength. Another is a bundle of twitch muscle. The third is completely unknown to me, but is exceptionally fit for a man of any age, let alone his. My fourth visiting instructor has whippet-like speed and the fifth is a surfer dude from South America. My point is that they all have unique physical characteristics have honed through years of intense training. Many of my students will avail of the seminars and I do believe they will share similar physical traits to my guests. Giving them the opportunity to train with these visiting sensei will, I hope, happily break pre-conceived ideas of what they believe karate should be whilst giving them patterns of movement and models of training that may suit them better than what is taught in my dojo.

http://www.lse.ac.uk/website-archive/newsAndMedia/videoAndAudio/channels/publicLecturesAndEvents/player.aspx?id=2234

THIRTY-TWO

Finding Zen in Venn

I am sure I live in a bubble. I don't have too much access to other groups, only the occasional Facebook stalking that is my go-to activity as bedtime approaches. However, I have convinced myself there is something of a paradigm shift taking place within the karate world. Old groups that once dominated the karate landscape are becoming marginalised at an exponential rate. Throughout my career I have had to be pragmatic, proactively and reactively dealing with what life throws at me. I see the writing on the wall for the old draconian groups and I have had this article in mind for many years. I eventually wrote it at the end of 2017.

In the classic 1974 book, *Zen and the Art of Motorcycle Maintenance*, Robert M. Pirsig describes in poetic detail one's innate ability to recognise quality. If you haven't read it, I implore you to do so. It is a fantastic novel that I read at a very impressionable age. The story and sentiment has stayed with me ever since. Pirsig introduces the idea that we all have an ability to identify and appreciate excellence and that it is fundamental to our artistic nature, whether that be martial or otherwise. Finding Zen in the everyday, he believes, is a worthy pursuit. I couldn't agree more.

A Venn diagram is a diagram that shows all possible logical relations between a finite collection of different sets. Such a diagram consists of multiple, normally overlapping, closed curves (usually circles) and each represents a set. So, how can we find Zen in Venn – and more importantly, what does this have to do with my day job?

For me, Photo 39 is a classic example of how karate groups have worked in the past. Different, mutually exclusive groups that never mix or meet. Over the years I have taught at a number of dojos that belong to this type of closed, protective groups; collectively attempting to live in isolation. My hosts, rebels within their chosen group, black sheep within the pack of white dogis, tell me in hushed breath about how they aren't really allowed to do this, to train with someone beyond their pale. Some associations are huge, others not so big, but they all have a similar characteristic – they are dictated over by a gatekeeper of knowledge, the person (or persons) at the top controlling course, gradings and competitions, even governing legitimacy, access and connections to the extended community. These gatekeepers, using a model and working in a paradigm of a bygone age, increasingly tighten their grip as their wards break free or unsettle the status quo. They produce a karate political landscape that can be characterised by the Venn diagram in Photo 39.

But does it have to be like this? What I have experienced over the last few years is a blurring of the lines, a contamination of groups and cross-pollination of karate-ka. The majority of my work is for the HDKI and as our policy is to insist that all our training events are open, we always have a number of guests, both training and teaching. There is a fluid exchange of ideas and as a result we find a number of individual karate-ka no longer fit into the old model of belonging to one group forever. I am Chief Technical Director of the HDKI, the proverbial buck stops with me. I am, however, also a member of Rick Hotton Sensei's Sunday Morning Keiko. There is no conflict of interest and, in fact, anyone who is interested in Rick Sensei's karate, whether you are HDKI or other, I recommend you join his growing community. I recently had an impressive *Shito Ryu* sensei teach at my dojo. Next year we have three big seminars in Dublin and on each of them there is a non-HDKI sensei making up part of the instructor team. My point is that for an increasing number of karate-kas, myself included, the martial arts landscape looks very similar to the Venn diagram in Photo 40.

Some, of course, will always continue to live within the

SHU-HA-RI – EVOLVING KARATE THOUGHTS

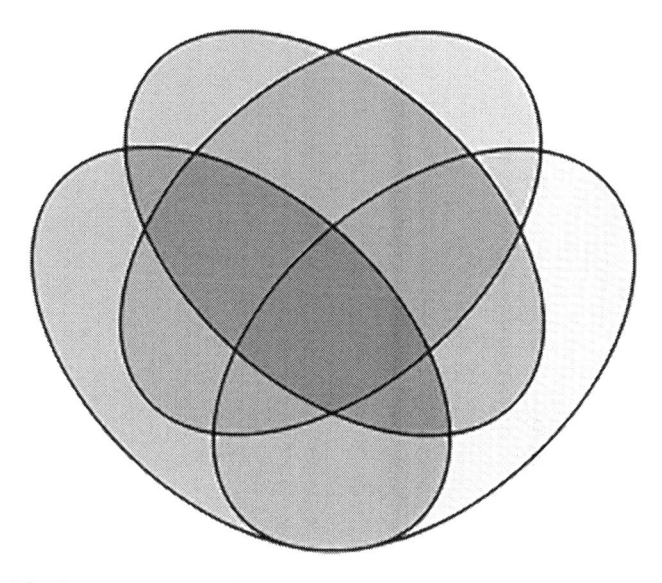

world of one group. Others predominantly live in one group, but dabble in others. And a further group live comfortably within a number of groups, finding their own way with guidance from a diverse variety of senior voices.

I can hear traditionalist screaming, 'What about loyalty?' Shouldn't we be forever loyal to our seniors, sensei and association? Well, for me, loyalty goes both ways. As sensei we must be providing a spectrum of ideas and voices to maximise our students' ability to progress along their personal karate journey. I have had the displeasure of hearing some instructors say they don't trust anyone else to teach their students. Apart from being the height of arrogance, I think this is an exercise in ego. What they are saying is that their karate is applicable to everyone, regardless of body type, ability and interest in the different aspects of karate. Limiting the input to students' karate journeys shows no loyalty to them. This is then starkly contrasted by insisting students show loyalty to the instructor by only training with them.

So this is how I see the karate world developing, an ever-increasingly complex Venn diagram of overlapping connections, fuelling innovation and karate adventures. That's why it's important to find the Zen in the Venn. Quality and one's innate ability to recognise it will become the guiding force when choosing where and whom to train with. Of course, quality can be very subjective. A young fighter developing their skills in the WKF arena doesn't want to train with me. A doorman wanting to gain specific functional skills for their job doesn't want to be refining the art of the martial. But karate is a broad church and having a community that looks like my second example of a Venn diagram can limit the continuous fracturing of our art and ensure the continued development through cooperation and integration of the quality we seek.

THIRTY-THREE

Oss-ification

This was the seventh article I wrote in the year since forming the HDKI. With it, I said my piece and set out clear goals and the ideals for the path I wished to take. I never wanted to form my own group, but by God I was determined to do the best possible job.

My feeling always settles somewhere between mild amusement and mild irritation when people feel the need to explain stuff to me through the lens of karate: 'Yeah, I'm an IT project manager – it's a bit like going into different dojos and setting up systems for managing students.' Or, 'I've just had a dressing-down by my line manager – it's a bit like being told off by your *sempai*.' Or even, 'I've just got divorced – it's a bit like when you were expelled from the WTKO!' 'Is that right?' I reply, really thinking, I know. I get the basic concepts of a world outside the dojo!

That said, I recently watched an interesting discussion between Russell Brand and Professor Brian Cox. In Brand's recent videos on YouTube, he has started interviewing, at length, great thinkers from a variety of backgrounds. This week's offering was the rock and roll star-turned-particle-physicist who was linking scientific thought to modern concepts of society, democracy and culture. He talked about complementarity and ossification. I listened with interest and couldn't help but think, That's exactly the same as karate … Maybe my friends are right to feed me their news and gossip through the filter of karate.

Complementarity is the state of being where one holds contradictory views. Sometimes described in the negative as cognitive dissonance, an example in physics would be describing light as being both a particle and a wave: both can't be right, but in the supernatural quantum world, it is. What Professor Cox cleverly did was relate this to modern politics and the state our various states, united or otherwise. He highlighted the incredible importance of politic discourse based on a variety of differing beliefs; the vitalness of challenging principles and having one's opinions tested; the importance of having a thesis and an antithesis in order to produce synthesis. He went on to give examples of how battles against the status quo have produce quantum leaps of progress. 'Who', he speculated, 'would have thought that the Brexit vote could actually lead to the election of the left-wing Jeremy Corbyn?' Good point, I thought.

He continued with the idea of ossification; the tendency towards or state of being modelled on a rigid, conventional or unimaginative condition. He argued that we must guard against being comfortable with the existing state of affairs; we must endeavour to strive forward, develop, innovate and investigate. He had some wonderful insights into global politics, but throughout the hour-long video I was constantly being brought back to our own incestuous world of karate.

Several years ago, I was teaching in the UK. Some JKS instructors, under the cover of dark, came to the course. It was great to see them, having had little to no contact with them since I left the group a few years previously. I taught, they trained and then we went to the pub afterwards. 'Your karate has really changed,' was their collective conclusion. Really? I thought. Since then, I have had similar comments and I've concluded that the radical change I made back in 2014 was the catalyst for this. Not the move to the WTKO itself, but the environment I found myself in. Certainly, Richard Amos' karate is very different from mine. I had my thesis of karate, he has his (which in many ways was the antithesis). From that exchange I think I found synthesis, which, I believe, took my karate forward. Since having to form the HDKI, I have refocused my desire to look for alternative ideas. Recently I have had the pleasure of training with Rick Jackson, Felipe Martin and Gary Redmond, now I am looking forward to welcoming Guy Brodeur and Mourad Saihai to my dojo in the coming months. My desire is to find new ideas and the more contradictory to my own, the better.

What I hope I have been doing for many years now is fighting ossification. We should be aware of people who are certain. Only saying '*oss*' will inevitably lead to ossification.

I remember when I first met Rick Hotton. I asked him about his pedigree: how did he become so good? 'I just spent a long time listening to my body,' he replied. Of course, he trained with many great instructors, listened to their ideas, studied their theses, then listened to his own body, examined the contradictions, revelled in the complementarity and produced synthesis.

On a physical level I never want to get analysis paralysis. I have always been fascinated by finding effective ways to train, effective ways to conceptualise what we do, why we do it and how best to go about it. I think the idea of complementarity is vital for any dojo or any group. Having contradictory voices produces innovation and prevents ossification. With that in mind ... back to YouTube for more insights by Russell Brand and his guests.

THIRTY-FOUR

Practical Karate

Okay – enough with the politics! At the beginning of 2018 I was asked to contribute to a book about the practical application of karate. I am not sure it will be published, so I reproduce it here for the first time. Karate has infiltrated every part of my life. Although I am unsure what the editor expected or wanted from me (the other contributors could be described as well-known karate tough guys), I gave my answer, trying to keep the liberal-left, hippy side of me as low-key as possible.

Oh no … What do I have to say about applying karate practically?

Back in 2010 I watched *Penn & Teller: Bullshit!*, where the two famous magicians debunked all martial arts as a fraud and not even a cost-effective way of defending oneself. I watched it thinking, fair enough. They made some very valid points.

Yet I have dedicated the last thirty-five years of my life to developing my own artistic version of this martial endeavour.

It must have some practical meaning. So, to respond to Messrs Penn & Teller's rebuke of martial arts and to answer the premise of this book, I think we first must decide why we start karate – after all, one person's practical application of karate may be another person's kung fu chopped liver. What are we, as practitioners, looking for in our open hand? Physical developments? Mental? Emotional or spiritual? Like any ambiguous or open-ended title, the possibilities are as wide as they are deep.

Physical developments

The obvious and, arguably, most valid practical effect of learning karate is the physical development a practitioner makes and their ability to defend themselves. But anyone who has trained for more than a handful of years knows that the actual shapes we make when learning technique are meaningless movements, having no relevance to the real world and real-life situations. When are we ever going to use a downward block or deliver a lunge punch? Critics of karate and other traditional martial arts view the endless repetition of these shapes as, at best, ineffective drills or, at worst, a pointless form that imbues the participants with dangerous levels of self-confidence. However, I have long abandoned the notion that I am learning karate as a set of movements or a recognisable thing. I'm not practising a martial art, I am becoming a martial artist. Through the superficial repetition of endless drills, we develop in two important ways: we build strength and flexibility and we increase our physical intelligence. Going through the *kyu* grades, we physically develop with the darkening of each colour of our belt. Done correctly, we don't learn karate, we become a karate-ka. Are we strong enough to defend ourselves against every foe we have the displeasure of meeting? Of course, not – there is always someone stronger than you. Are we stronger than 99 per cent of our similar demographic? Do we reach our physical potential? Are we fitter, stronger and more kinaesthetically aware than our peer group? Yes we are!

For me, becoming a karate-ka is the most practical application of practicing karate. Do the karate technique and shapes we practise work? No, of course not! How can we ever expect a rising block to be effective as a defence against a drunken thug in the streets? But that's not the point. The strength, fitness and physical intelligence that countless hours of training bestows upon us increases our chances of blocking, parrying or dodging said drunken attack. We can't hope to defend ourselves from all adversaries but we can hope to increase the likelihood of success to as close to 100 per cent as reasonably possible.

Some instructors decide to shortcut the system and believe that if the ultimate aim is to defend oneself from a haymaker in the street, then let's solely practise defences against more realistic scenarios. I understand their point and acknowledge their rationale – above all else, karate is a broad church. That said, I believe the strict regime of physical movement that *kihon* and kata forces us down will ultimately give us freedom of movement. Once you learn to micromanage every muscle group and the minutiae of every physical exchange, then your ability to take control of situations greatly increases. Karate is a physical language. Like any language, we must start with the building blocks of communication: vocabulary, syntax, grammar, *kihon*, kumite, kata. At first, communication will be stilted and cumbersome but with practice, a level of fluency will be gained. After many years of constant development, the language becomes natural, done without thought. We can even see how that language can become uniquely our own, with idiosyncratic usage of idioms and intonation, *tokui waza* and timing. Whether defending oneself verbally or physically, the more fluent you are, the better. Becoming a martial artist is like learning a foreign language whilst trying to develop a native speaker's skill. Full of nuance, poise, skill and composure, a true karate-ka will reach a state of *mushin* and practically apply karate effortlessly, fluently, naturally.

Before we move on to the less physical aspects of karate, it must be noted that all karate-ka walk a fine line between focusing on the function of karate and leaving the art behind, whilst others focus on the form of karate, allowing it to become close to a dance. Within all form there must be function and with all function there must be form. The constant nudging and tweaking of our practice is essential to fulfilling one's potential.

Emotional developments

I remember, many years ago now, sitting on the steps of the church that was the centrepiece of my university campus. Twenty years earlier students had been allowed to vote on whether to build a swimming pool or a church. They held the vote at 7 am on a Sunday morning and suffice to say, I found myself on steps of a church almost exclusively used to hold end-of-year exams. It was the start of my finals, a series of exams that, over the next two weeks, would see the culmination of my three years of degree-level study. I sat with my head in my hands, allowing the sun to warm my neck.

'Jeez mate, are you all right? Don't let the pressure get to you!' A friend had sidled up to me to offer some words of comfort.

'Oh, no, I'm fine ... I was just in Scotland all weekend,

training. I only got back late last night and I'm knackered.'
He looked at me with a mixture of confusion and disdain and
walked off.

I think my little anecdote illustrates two things: my
complete lack of ability to take my university studies seriously
and, emotionally, how karate can have significant practical
benefits. I often think karate makes the rest of life easy.
Whilst my university contemporaries were fretting over finals
and their ejection from campus into the real world, I would
always think, How bad can it be? I have to fight *sempai* in the
dojo this evening. I believe that we start with the physical in
karate, learning to control every facet of our body. At a point,
some sooner, some later, we must deal with the emotional
aspect of our being. Facing a tough squad training, entering
a competition or simply walking into the dojo can be stressful
enough to produce a vomit-inducing reaction. As karate-ka,
we have all faced and faced down these situations. We must
learn how to read our opponents and in doing so we learn
how to read ourselves. Consequently, we develop a level
of emotional control that percolates throughout our lives.
Starting a new job? Well, no one will try to hit you. Having
financial difficulties? Well, at least I can still do what I love
– train. Facing the daily drudgery of life? What drudgery?
Life is challenging, thrilling and exciting with constant
karate adventures. Best-case scenario, we develop a level of
emotional intelligence and awareness of people that again
raises us above the norms of our peer group – we maximise our
potential, which has layer upon layer of practical applications.

WELL-BEING ADVANTAGES

Whilst at the above-mentioned university, I read anthropology.
I do remember a few things I studied. One lesson that comes

to me now is how, over the years, well-being and happiness has been defined, studied and quantified. There are two significant factors, presuming all basic human requirements are satisfied (food, shelter, clothing etc.) that contribute to one's happiness. One is a sense of community, both micro and macro. The other is a sense of development and progress as we face conquerable challenges.

With community, it has been proven time and time again that people feel happiest when they are part of a close-knit group, when they have a peer group that is supportive and regulatory, challenging them when appropriate, supporting them when needed. But these micro connections are only part of the equation. Communities also need macro connections, links to a larger world, facilitating a greater sense of being and a wider connection to a bigger world of ideas, trends and paradigms. My dojo is a small, intimate family and it makes me happy. Belonging to the wider community to which the dojo is affiliated brings that happiness into greater focus and augments an already enriched karate life.

The second element of happiness is the ability to progress in one's chosen activity. Monotony is the bedrock of a life unrealised. The endless refining of technique and the esoteric nature of karate provide a vehicle whereby any practitioner can forever be challenged, overcoming the metaphorical walls that we often hit and revel in the 'ah-ha' moments that development provide – just when we feel we understand what karate is, a whole new level, area or challenge is revealed to us. I hope most karate-ka are part of their own dojo family, which, in turn, is connected to a wider community. As long as it isn't dysfunctional, then karate can practically help build happiness and well-being.

Shu-Ha-Ri – Evolving Karate Thoughts

Mental advantages

Recent studies have shown that physical movement facilitates cognitive ability. Remember being in the classroom and being told to sit still? Anyone with children will confirm their passion for fidgeting. Do you go for a walk to mull over a problem you are facing? It turns out that the act of physical movement helps to process the various strands of information you have taken on board. The mind/body connection is very real and modern science is starting to realise and quantify such connections.

Another important aspect of mental development is that the more information that one needs to process, the longer time seems to take. Remember how a summer holiday from school stretched out in front of you like a lifetime? Or even now when, after a two-week holiday, upon returning home it seems like you have been away for an age? This is down to being exposed to new and different stimuli. The mind works overtime in processing such experiences resulting in a perceived slowing-down of time – ask anyone who has been in a car crash if the sudden turn of unfortunate events felt like it went on for ever. But what does this have to do with the practical application of karate?

Firstly, any physical activity will help to create a healthy mind and body, but karate takes this a step further. In martial arts there are innumerable possibilities played out in countless situations. No two fights are the same, no two performances of kata are identical and no two techniques in the repetitions of *kihon* should share all the same nuances. In some sports the *Yips* can often plague the professional elite, affecting athletes in cricket, baseball, golf and even darts. It can be seen in many sports where the same, simply physical movement is repeated to a high degree of accuracy. It is believed that the highly defined neurological network that produces the intricate movement simply breaks down. Karate-ka could never get the *Yips*. We are constantly laying down new pathways as we discover the hidden depths of karate. As a result, the plasticity of our minds is maintained. We aim to be neither stiff in our body nor mind, producing an adaptability that can be applied practically anywhere. Added to this is the constant processing of new stimuli; a lifetime of a karate-ka can be stretched out by a satisfying degree by the constant presence of new challenges in one's life.

Can some of what I have highlighted above be gained from other worthy pursuits? Of course. Does every karate-ka benefit in the ways I have described? Of course not. We live in a challenging world populated by imperfect dojos with sensei that demonstrate none of the aforementioned qualities. Some dojos don't practise kumite, some karate-ka don't build up a sweat, some communities are controlling and dysfunctional. Living a life constantly on the lookout for danger will conclude like a damp squib. Spending a lifetime training in a dojo with no sense of danger is equivalent to dancing in one's pyjamas. But in the right circumstances, with the right checks and balances and with the right knowledge, I believe that karate can have far-reaching and exceptionally positive practical applications, which start with the physical and spread throughout the spectrum of human existence.

THIRTY-FIVE

Karate-Do

I was sitting on a barstool at the Hill Valley Golf Club. It was the lunch break between the gruelling morning and afternoon session of the bi-monthly black and brown belt courses that Ishii Sensei ran in Whitchurch, Shropshire. I was eighteen years old. I'd just finished high school and had decided to take a year out to work, save and go to Japan a year hence. In front of me I had a plate of sandwiches as well as chips, which were doused with copious amounts of salt and vinegar, and a pint of blackcurrant and soda water. I was eagerly consuming the lot – the breakfast of champions.

'So, Scott ... what do you want to do with karate?' Bob Sensei, a very senior member of Ishii Sensei's UK-based group had wandered to the bar and spotted me at the far end.

'I want to be the best in the world,' I said confidently through a fizzy mouthful of blackcurrant soda and ham sandwich, 'but I'll settle for being the best I can be.'

'Where did you read that?' Bob Sensei sounded sceptical.

'Err ... I didn't ... I just thought of it.'

Bob raised an eyebrow, Spock-like, and walked off.

Actually, that's not what happened. Here's what happened.

Shu-Ha-Ri – Evolving Karate Thoughts

I was sitting at the end of the bar, underneath the TV. It was dark and I wanted to be invisible for a while. I was stuffing down as much sugar and as many carbs that I could get into me in anticipation of another mental, energy-depleting session in the afternoon. I saw Bob Sensei wandering to the bar, so put my head down, suddenly finding fascination in the assembly of my ham sandwich.

'So, Scott … what do you want to do with karate?'

'I want to be the best in the world …' *You arrogant PRICK! How can you get away with that? Ishii Sensei has only just started remembering your name. Up until the last seminar you were just Little Boy from Yorkshire! For fuck's sake, say something else – redeem yourself!* '… but I'll settle for being the best I can be.'

空手道とは? (What is karate-do?) It was one of the two dozen questions I had to answer as part of the written report for the instructors' course. There was a rumour within the headquarters that oscillated between urban myth and a strong possibility of being absolutely true that one particularly sluggish trainee instructor simply answered 空手は蹴り技と突き技 (Karate is kicking and punching). What could his sensei and sempai say to disagree?

My response to the question has been lost, not so much in time but in technological development. The floppy disks on which all my answers resideno longer have any use other than as drink coasters. So I will attempt to answer the question one more time.

Like an onion, karate has endless layers, each claiming to be the most important depending on whom you talk to. What is karate to me? To me personally? To me professionally? Emotionally? Physically? Psychologically? You get the idea. Beginning to answer that question comprehensively will ultimately prove impossible within this short article. It is my job, my profession, my hobby, my passion, my raison d'être. I can only deteriorate into talking in generalities, giving broad brushstrokes in the hope the reader can get the gist of my thoughts and feeling. My days are filled either with thinking up *kihon* and kumite combinations that represent a concept I am working on at the time, or sentence structures that concisely and precisely convey the thoughts of someone who was once describe as 'semi-illiterate' by a rather formidable history teacher. And, when bored with both these activities, I try to create gags that I can crow-bar in between the delivery of the two. In the swirl of this physical and cerebral activity, I optimistically hope to find meaning within the art to which I have dedicated my life. But even these brief glimpses of a truth meander, fluctuate and coalesce into and then disintegrate out of existence. My relationship with karate is dynamic.

Yamaguchi Takeshi Sensei, a *sempai* of mine from back in the JKS days, once said to me that in karate there are no ends, only new beginnings. Starting karate, we begin a journey. Achieving black belt, we set out on a new expedition. Becoming an instructor, opening a dojo, creating our own group; these are all new challenges. Within the dojo, searching for the minutiae of detail within each technique endlessly reveals how little we know. Moving from the superficial to the profound reveals that in many ways karate is esoteric – only when we have one level of understanding do we realise the existence of other higher levels.

Karate physically embodies Will Durant's belief that 'education is a progressive discovery of our own ignorance'. Karate is no longer a set of movements to learn, a set of principles to study, but a journey to take.

As I reach my mid-forties, my new beginning is finding a

way to sustainably train with a body fighting atrophy. In the next decade I hope to discover a new role as I take a step back from my hectic schedule, encouraging younger instructors to travel, teach and spread the world. And that is what I see now; who knows what new challenges I will face in my fifties and sixties?

Ultimately, I am slowly developing my way in karate, my karate-do. No longer practising a martial art, I am (hopefully) becoming a martial artist. What do I mean by this? Who knows? The meaning is often intangible to me; sometimes I have it, other times I don't. However, this is what I happen to believe right now: karate helps to create balance in my life. It gives me self-confidence, physically, emotionally, psychologically. More importantly, it keeps me grounded. With every fight I lose, or bruise I gain, or ache I nurse, or failure I experience, the narcissistic side of me is beaten into submission. No narcissist can every truly become an artist because they refuse to allow themselves to be vulnerable. They may be able to paint the best pictures, write the greatest novels or sculpt the finest statues, but they only become artists when their work is published, shown or revealed for the world to see. The artist is born from the vulnerability of their creation, like a parent knowing a little part of their heart permanently resides in their haphazard child. By becoming a martial artist, we have to realise both our strengths and weaknesses. We should be guided by our ego and insecurities, our friends and critics, our lovers and haters. We can exist in a feedback loop that constantly delivers a peer-reviewed critique on our efforts so far. Positive and negative reinforcement is allowed to seep in, either inflating or deflating the ego until balance is achieved. Sometimes I ramble off course, one way or another, but training brings me back to a balanced state. This is the constant in my life.

Is this true for everyone? Of course, not. Rick Hotton Sensei believes karate is about love. Yahara Mikio Sensei believes that karate is *ikken hissatsu* (one strike, one kill). Everyone is different, everyone must find their own *do* in karate. However, for me, physical, emotional and psychological balance has always been my objective – well, balance with a slight imbalance. Being open to criticism, allowing myself to be vulnerable, finding ways to be collaborative not only shackles the narcissistic ego, it also gives me a healthy insecurity, urging me on, forever refining. I must learn and adapt in order to survive: in the karate world change is inevitable, progress is optional. I feel it is the natural consequence of realising I know nothing and is a path to a life fulfilled. However …

Several years after I returned from Japan I was at my friend Tony's wedding. I greeted old university alumni who I hadn't seen for many years and introduced myself to other guests I had never met. Tony had spent three years travelling the world and many of his worldwide network had made the trip to the UK for the celebration. Over drinks, one new acquaintance asked me what I did for a living.

'I teach karate.'

'Wow, where do you teach?'

'Well, different places …'

'Like, you have a few schools?'

'No … I teach all over the world.' Prompted by the look of surprise of the assembled group, I elaborated: 'I was in Japan for many years, I completed the instructors' course and became the fifth foreigner in about fifty years to graduate. Now I travel and teach all over the world.'

'Wow!' was the collective response.

Next to me, a rather distinguished, well-groomed chap was enthusiastically taking it all in. Raul had flown in from Mexico

City the day before and was someone Tony had spoken about a lot. The same questioner turned to him and asked the same question.

'I teach also.'

'Where do you teach?'

'We have our own high school in Mexico City.'

'Your own school?' Everyone was intrigued.

'Well … my family business is fairly successful. So, a few years back I re-trained as a teacher. We now run a school and I take in poor children from the area, educate them for free, give them a fighting chance and hope they will go on to become productive members of society. It is very rewarding,' he concluded, almost as an afterthought.

Wow, I thought. And at the end of the day, what is karate-do?

Just kicking and punching.

About the Author

Scott began Ju-Jitsu in Liverpool, UK at the age of five. Fearing separation anxiety, he decided to follow his parents to Yorkshire, when he was ten years old. There, he started Karate and has been training, with varying degrees of intensity, ever since. He moved to Japan in 1997, completed the JKS Instructors' Course and set up the JKS GB & Ireland, all of which has been covered extensively in his two best-selling books, *Karate Stupid* and *Karate Clever*. Based in Dublin, Ireland since 2002, he is now Chief Technical Director or the HDKI and continues to teach, train and write.

Tetsuhiko Asai 10th Dan showing Scott how it's done – Tokyo, Autumn 2001

Printed in Great Britain
by Amazon